STREET KIDS
AND OTHER PLAYS

MORE WILDSIDE CLASSICS

STREET KIDS AND OTHER PLAYS

by

BRIO BURGESS

Edited by

Daryl F. Mallett

WILDSIDE PRESS

STREET KIDS AND OTHER PLAYS

This edition published in 2006 by Wildside Press, LLC.
www.wildsidepress.com

CONTENTS

These plays contain numerous routines composed
of jazz songs and soft ballet...routines that
can be presented or suggested in mime. The
characters are surreal, the dances idealized
versions of reality...

PREFACE

"A beggar's book outworths a noble's blood."
--Buckingham's speech in Act I of
Henry VIII, by William Shakespeare

The works in this volume are snapshots of the worlds in which some children live. The stories are cameos of their lives and were written over a span of thirty years in many different parts of the United States.

"Lost City Nights" is a picture of life in the American Gulag. It is a stark, bleak portrait depicting the miseries of a street addict who has to struggle for illegal medication to take away the pain of having to be. Ruby and Reaper are lovers, but they are so deeply distracted that they can't just get married and have children to resolve their relationship. They can't settle down...there's nowhere for them to rest. This first play follows them from the day they meet through the establishment of the patterns of their lives together over time. Written in various parts of the U.S., from 1965-95.

In "Street Kids," we meet Ruby and Reaper again, seeking shelter with Merk and The Shades, the gang that rules Styx Alley, as the storm of revolution blazes up from underground on a hot summer night. This small family now has a child, Ebony, who must share the fortunes of the couple and the others who come into their lives. Their very existence is illegal. They have to keep on running, living as outlaws. This is their story, a tragic love story filled with black humor. People caught in a life without hope, they're guilty of innumerable felonies twenty-four hours a day. Written, revised and performed in Albany, New York, from 1984-93.

"Rooftops" (also known as "Broadway Blues") is the tale of people like those who used to hang out in a place called Wino Park on Sixth Street in San Francisco, California. This park, no longer in existence, had been created with donated funds for the purpose of "the preservation of people." In the middle of its brick landscaping was a plaque inscribed with the names of famous substance abusers such as Billie Holliday, Janis Joplin, Charlie Parker, Jimi Hendrix and Jeanne Eagels. This play is a meditation on the thoughts and interactions of the kinds of people who may have sat on the benches and relaxed in the atmosphere that had been created especially for their use. Written in Albany, New York in 1982.

"Space Visions" takes place in the future, as seen through the eyes of a young artist struggling to understand her era's place in history at a time when deep questions about the way humanity lives must be answered if the species is to survive. "The Writer's Song" from this play, appearing on the back cover behind the self-portrait of Lawrence Ferlinghetti, was distributed in audio to twenty-one countries around the world. Written in California and New York, 1971-75.

LOST CITY NIGHTS

This is a portrait of the relationship between Ruby, a dancer turned street addict, and her boyfriend Reaper as they go from first meeting to the bleak reality of a lifestyle below the law, chasing the illegal substance twenty-four hours a day. Their tragic love story projects the humor and pathos of life on the edge without hope. It is this lifestyle, this subterranean existence, that the play addresses.

> talking 'bout the birth of beat, in the season of the heat
> everybody was going to school, learning the golden
> rule
>
> do unto others as you would have them do unto you if you
> wanna know the secret of the cool...
>
> there's a forbidden lake in Shangrila, where the Dalai Lama
> and Milarepa went to meditate in a cave where they
> could hallucinate without interruption, and fast in silent
> contemplation

CAST:

RUBY   Dancer, 21

LADY CRYSTAL   Dancer/cocktail waitress, 21

REAPER   35 year old dude

CANDY   RUBY's brother, 19

DRAC   Bartender, 30

CLOWN   Broken-down wrestler/nightclub
                                                    bouncer, 40

MR. TEDDY BEAR   Eccentric with gold necklaces,
     fancy three-piece silk or leather suit with
               red vest and shoes to match his red
                                              handkerchief

THE BOYS   A group of three or four young men in
      their 20s, dressed as rock stars; long hair,
                                       lots of jewelry

GIRL IN GREEN ARMY PARKA   17

COUPLE   Boy, 18/Girlfriend, 17

HOT DOG PALACE COUNTERMAN   Lean fellow, late 30s

SETS:

Act 1, Scene 1   The Halloween Nightclub
Act 1, Scene 2   The Halloween Nightclub
Act 2, Scene 1   20th Century Mardi Gras Street
Act 3, Scene 1   The Psychedelic Pad
Act 3, Scene 2   The Broken Haiku Stash Pad
Act 4, Scene 1   The Almost Never-Ending Concrete
                                       City Sidewalk
Act 4, Scene 2   The Relief Office
Act 4, Scene 3   The Hot Dog Palace
Act 4, Scene 4   In front of Hot Dog Palace
                                   and Caffe Trieste
Epilogue   In front of Caffe Trieste

ACT I

Scene 1:

The nightclub, once known as The Red Balloon, now known as The Dead Balloon or The Halloween Nightclub, on a rainy big city night in San Francisco about twenty years ago. The aura is that of a subdued, garish, Halloweenesque dream sequence. A slide, the entrance from the street, is at the left of the bar. A dance platform is at the right of the bar.

RUBY, dressed in tassels and spangles, dances on the platform. Her bumps and grinds are performed in slow motion. She greatly resembles a child making feeble attempts to be suggestive. The jukebox is playing. CLOWN, the nightclub's bouncer, hangs out inside and outside the club, going back and forth, checking the action. DRAC, the bartender, dressed as a vampire, with rubber fangs protruding from his upper lip, is mixing drinks for LADY CRYSTAL, a girl dressed in a tuxedo, top hat, tails and spats, who is wandering around picking up empty glasses from the tables.

MR. TEDDY BEAR is sitting at a round table surrounded by a group of BOYS dressed like rock stars. They have pitchers of beer and wooden bowls of popcorn and pretzels on the table in front of them. MR. TEDDY BEAR rises from his seat, approaches LADY CRYSTAL, says something, returns to the table. LADY CRYSTAL looks over at them, smiles negatively, returns to the bar, as the clock approaches the hour before closing time. It chimes with big "Dong!"s. A few scattered customers are visible.

REAPER, dressed in alternating hues of pink and orange, a Little Lord Fauntleroy costume arrayed tastefully and carelessly, comes in. He sits at the bar, orders a drink, looks around, leans towards LADY CRYSTAL, lounging against the bar.

> REAPER
> You doing a takeoff on Dietrich or something?

LADY CRYSTAL smiles indifferently and goes over to stand by the fireplace. The lights are changing, the other customers are beginning to leave. MR. TEDDY BEAR again approaches LADY CRYSTAL, introduces himself, hands her his card. She ignores him; he puts it into her pocket. LADY CRYSTAL takes it out, looks at it, then returns with him to his table.

The music in the background becomes louder. REAPER, the only customer at the bar now, turns to watch RUBY dance.

> REAPER
> Come on, honey! Put some life in it! Snap it more...bump it a little!

REAPER is drunk. RUBY attempts feebly to snap it. REAPER turns back to DRAC.

> REAPER
> Where do you get these dames?
> (looks back at RUBY with compassion)
> Ah, maybe she's tired. She sure doesn't know how to snap it.

> DRAC
> Poor kid has lots of problems. Wanted a job. Clown found her on the street one night. He felt sorry for her, got her something to eat, brought her over here. She's better than nothing!

                    REAPER
The girl should have more energy.
She's too young to be so tired. I
work hard all day and I could do
that stuff better.

                    DRAC
She's a good kid, but got lots of
problems, like so many of 'em
these days. Been through the
mill, turned upside-down, inside-
out by everyone she's ever met.
        (leans toward REAPER confidentially)
        We'll have to let her go
soon, though. This place just
isn't making it.

                    REAPER
Oh, yeah? Well, gimme another.
I'll contribute to the lost cause
of derelict dancers in derelict
bars.

CLOWN comes down the slide and limps over to
lean against the bar. He resembles a paunchy
wrestler, is dressed in a soiled red-and-white
satin circus suit. His face is painted white in
the style of Marcel Marceau's street mime. He
walks with a limp.

                    CLOWN
It's raunchy as hell out there.

                    DRAC
(setting up drink for CLOWN)
Not any better in here...

                    CLOWN
How's Ruby doing?
    (looks up and watches RUBY)
        Looks kind of heavy tonight.

                    DRAC
              (indicates REAPER)
       That dude seems to enjoy it,
       though.

                    CLOWN
       Wonder how he'd do up there?

                    DRAC
               (with a wink)
       Why don't you ask him? Might make
       him thirsty for something besides
       beer!

                    CLOWN
       (shrugs shoulders, sips his drink)
        Okay, here goes nothing.
            (limps over to REAPER)
            Hear you were giving our girl
       a bad time.

                    REAPER
       Well, look at her. She's kind of
       a bum, as far as dancing goes.

                    CLOWN
       Why don't you go up and join her?
       `I'll buy you a drink to make you
       feel it.

                    REAPER
            Ah...
       (hesitates; is about to leave but reconsiders)
            Okay. Bourbon on the rocks.

                    CLOWN
               (to DRAC)
       Set the gent up, Drac.

DRAC fixes REAPER's drink. CLOWN goes over to
the jukebox and puts on something with drum
beats in it. DRAC gives the drink to REAPER,
who gulps it down, slides off the stool, and
saunters up the stairs of the platform. When on

the platform, he goes into a slow twisting sort of motion, following RUBY who, where before she was performing as though in a trance, begins to complement his movements.

> REAPER
> Hi, honey!

> RUBY
> (seems to notice him for the first time)
> Please don't talk!

REAPER and RUBY relate to the music and to each other. DRAC and CLOWN watch.

> CLOWN
> Well, hit me again so I can go out and see how the world's doing.

> DRAC
> Try to bring in some live ones.

DRAC gives CLOWN another drink, which he gulps down.

> CLOWN
> Okay.

CLOWN gets up, puts change in the jukebox, presses some selections, and feebly makes his way back up the slide stairs to the outside world.

Lights dim until only a spotlight remains on REAPER and RUBY dancing.

> FADE TO BLACK

Scene 2:

It is almost closing time at The Halloween Nightclub. RUBY and REAPER are sitting at the bar. REAPER is buying her a drink.

>   REAPER
>   (to DRAC)
> Give us two more!
>   (turns to RUBY)
>   How long you been working
> here?

>   RUBY
>   (tired and bored)
> Couple weeks.

>   REAPER
> You with anybody?

>   RUBY
> Clown got me the job.
>   (looks directly at REAPER)
>   I'm married to a monkey.

>   REAPER
> You mean a Swatza?

>   RUBY
> I wish I did!

>   REAPER
> Don't you wanna go someplace else?

>   RUBY
> I've got to wait for Clown.

>   REAPER
> Why? You aren't with him, are
> you?

>   RUBY
> He's my mother!

>   REAPER
> You're putting me on...

DRAC comes over to them, looks at REAPER.

                    DRAC
You want another? It's almost
closing time.

                    REAPER
                 (gestures)
Yeah, might as well. Two more.

DRAC sets up drinks; REAPER slams one. CLOWN
comes tiredly down the slide. He limps to the
end of the bar to survey the situation. His
makeup is beginning to wear off. DRAC sets up a
drink for him. RUBY sees CLOWN.

                    RUBY
                 (to REAPER)
Just a minute. I'll be right
back.
(gets up; hurries over to CLOWN)

                    REAPER
Where you goin'?

                    CLOWN
                 (to RUBY)
You know where it is.
   (RUBY hugs CLOWN; exits)

                    REAPER
                 (to DRAC)
What's with her?
   (drinks second drink)

                    DRAC
Crazy.
   (twirls finger by head)
      Probably had to go to the
john.

DRAC shrugs, goes through the motions of closing
up, wiping off bottles, the bar, etc.

>   REAPER
> Might as well give me another.
> Will she be out soon?

CLOWN gets up and limps off in direction of
RUBY's exit.

>   CLOWN
> Go'night, Drac!

>   DRAC
> Yeah! Take it easy, now!

CLOWN exits.

>   DRAC
>   (looks at REAPER sadly)
> You want one for the road, kid?

>   REAPER
> Yeah, might as well.

RUBY comes back in, dressed in a Peter Pan
costume composed of green tights, army parka,
shoes. She is strangely exuberant, hurries up
to the bar, stands beside REAPER.

>   RUBY
> You waited for me, baby! Hey, you
> wanna do something?

REAPER looks about, as in a fog. He is
surprised by her change in attitude.

>   REAPER
> What happened to you?

>   RUBY
> Come on. Let's blow this joint.
> I know lots of places, depends on
> what you want.
>   (cheerfully)
> You wanna tell me about
> yourself?

                    REAPER
Okay, baby, you asked for it.
Come on, let's go!

REAPER and RUBY exit. DRAC continues wiping the
glasses. CLOWN enters in street clothes, limps
up to bar.

                    CLOWN
She make out?

                    DRAC
Won't know 'til tomorrow. Hope
she doesn't blow it.

                    CLOWN
We'll probably have to get rid of
Ruby. I talked to another little
chick tonight. Same story, wants
a job. Streets are full of 'em!

                    DRAC
            (laughing gently)
At least we never have to worry
about getting a dancer.

                    CLOWN
Yeah.

                            FADE TO BLACK

            END ACT I

ACT II

A surreal, iridescent, luminous, electrically
vibrating 20th-century street. Both sides of
the street are lined with boutiques, import
shops, restaurants, bars, nightclubs, cafés,
antique shops, art galleries, and on one side
there is a park. The storefronts are as old
frontier town facades, painted for optical
effect, seeming to weave in and out. Lights of
many colors are flashing over the hanging, life-
sized, chromatically hued paper cut-outs of
people, costumed with painted line suggestions
which flap sadly like forgotten scarecrows.
These abandoned crepe mannequins, paper shadows
portraying representatives of all aspects of
life, are the props of this multicolored
sidewalk stage. The mood is that of a carnival
midway, only, instead of booths of kewpie dolls,
darts, balloons, rifle shooting and penny
pitching at each corner, in front of every
doorway there are scattered among the floating
paper cut-outs, two ragged specimens of once-
humanity. They're the hucksters, the hawkers of
the carnival, guarding their turf, while calling
out a general mantra of acid, speed, pot, acid,
speed, pot...occasionally an offer of STP, THC,
hashish, coke, or smack is heard. The air is
stereoized with symphonic city sounds of
foghorns, freeway rumblings and occasional
offkey, improvised flute notes.

RUBY, with frosted hair, bare feet, ragged mini-
dress, clutching a fistful of money, is weaving
her way in and out of the hanging, flapping
paper crowd. She goes up to one of the
storefronts, knocks on the door, gets no answer.
She continues down the street, nodding to the
carnival barkers. REAPER--now dressed as a drug

dealer, a 21st-century version of Simon Legree,
in green elf boots, purple velvet bell-bottoms,
purple vest, green Tom Jones silk shirt, many
rings, jewelry and white Panama hat--emerges
from the bookstore, also clutching a wad of
money and sacks of books. RUBY rushes toward
him. REAPER wearily stops. They walk down the
street together. The carnival barkers are
singing the mantra...acid, speed, pot, acid,
speed, pot...as though it were a Brechtian dirge
performed by a chorus from Hell.

                    RUBY
          You know, honey, the little
          greenies, or maybe strawberries,
          or bennies, or anything...

                    REAPER
          We'll see.

They look through a drugstore window.

                    REAPER
          You want cigarettes? You hungry?
          Thirsty?

RUBY shakes her head. The two stall, milling
around, walk further along. Occasionally REAPER
will stop and mumble something to one of the
barkers. RUBY looks at dresses in windows as
they weave their way through the crepe-paper
mannequins. The barkers become fewer in number
as they make their way down the street. Those
who remain are huddled in doorways as shadows or
ghosts, their faces deathly white. REAPER still
stops to speak with one here and there while
RUBY follows him.

They continue down the street. One of the
storefronts is a delicatessen, signified by a
sign saying so. Through the glass door and
windows are seen plastic-topped tables.
Hippyish people are sitting at the tables. Some
are talking, some staring. The mood is that of
congested boredom. CANDY, a youth, tall and

ragged, is going from table to table panhandling. REAPER and RUBY sit at one of the vacant tables outside. The youth comes to their table.

                    CANDY
You got any spare change?

                    REAPER
          (reaches into his pocket)
Not this time.

                    RUBY
              (looks up)
Candy!
              (to REAPER)
     This is my brother.
     (pulls at CANDY's sleeve)
          Sit down, baby. What are you
doing?
              (to REAPER again)
     This is my brother.

                    REAPER
We've met.

                    RUBY
              (to CANDY)
What have you been doing? That's
obvious. Where are you staying?

                    CANDY
Everywhere. I'm a citizen of the
world, inhabitant of the fifth
largest planet in the solar
system, and a member of the
universe. How are you?

                    RUBY
Think we could get a joint?

                    REAPER
              (to CANDY)
That redhead was a lousy lay.

                    CANDY
                  (to RUBY)
I had some gold, but we used it
and gave the rest away.

                    REAPER
Hey, Candy. Does your old lady
still roll like a pro?

                    CANDY
We've gotten one of those
machines, streamlined weed, cross-
wired with speed.

                    RUBY
Hey, Candy, why don't we go blow?

                    CANDY
Oh, well, the old lady. I'll ask
her, we have to wait. She's
uptight, relatives are visiting...
You wanna drop some acid?

                    REAPER
We've got some real good smack for
a change...

                    CANDY
I did that already.

                    RUBY
                  (to REAPER)
Hey, baby, you gotta quarter for
some beer?

                    REAPER
                 (ignores her)
I sure could use some downers...

                    CANDY
My old man's into a few darvons, a
few phenobarbitals. I gotta take
eight or ten of 'em just to get to
sleep at night...

REAPER gets up and wanders away from the table, hands in his pockets, looks up at the sky, kicks a can, goes back to the table, sits, starts talking to CANDY.

> REAPER
> Say, Candy, did you say somethin' about downers? Somethin' about phenob?

> CANDY
> Yeah. We can get that. But first my sister said something about a quarter for a beer. My old lady's waitin' for her check, and I've gotta be a little loaded if we're gonna split.

CANDY looks forlorn as he focuses on the flapping, passing, sadly hanging crepe-paper silhouettes. He gets up and panhandles them as he exits, in dance pantomime to the background of old time music in rock time...a jazz version of "Buddy, Can You Spare a Dime?"

> RUBY
> You wanna come?

> REAPER
> Yeah, let's go get stoned.

REAPER and RUBY get up and bop out. The crepe-paper people are hanging in less number. They are colored in varying shades of grey flannel and portray varying moods of early morning grogginess, hurrying-not-to-be-late stumbliness, robotic automatized briskness. Grey-blue hues illustrate the mood, as symphonic city sounds of foghorns, freeway rumblings and footfall stumblings stereoize the air.

FADE TO BLACK

END ACT II

ACT III

Scene 1:

A large room. The windows and walls are covered with rock band posters. Mobiles and kinetics, sculptural structures, hang from the ceiling. MR. TEDDY BEAR is in bed in the center of the room, surrounded by antiques, horror comic books, empty Coke bottles, Egyptian scarabs, numerous periodicals, mechanical war and monster toys. Benson & Hedges cigarette boxes rise as towers from the corners of the room.

DRAC, the bartender, is lounging in a velvet chair. CLOWN is sitting on the floor in one of the corners, scowling. He is hung up for his money. REAPER and RUBY come in. RUBY sits on the edge of the bed. REAPER and MR. TEDDY BEAR affect poses and routines reminiscent of 1930s' Edward G. Robinson, Jimmy Cagney gangster movies. They're talking dope-dealing and enjoying it. The actions can be improvised, in mime, while music plays in the background.

> MR. TEDDY BEAR
> (looks at CLOWN)
> If Candy doesn't show, we'll have
> to make good!

DRAC gets up from his chair, goes over and sits on floor near RUBY. He tries to talk to her to see if she's stoned or not.

> DRAC
> (points to table)
> What is that on the table?

> RUBY
> (distractedly watching everyone else)
> A stick.

REAPER is pacing up and down the room, gesturing wildly. MR. TEDDY BEAR is not reacting; he does not alter his physical position other than to roll joints with a mechanical gadget to make them look like real cigarettes.

> DRAC
> (to RUBY)
> That's a burnt match!

> RUBY
> (assumes an academic pose)
> If that were a burnt match, it would be dead, but if it's a stick, it can still serve some purpose. It still can be. It was once a match, but it is no longer a match. Therefore, it is something else!

REAPER, MR. TEDDY BEAR and DRAC look at each other and wink. CLOWN keeps scowling.

> MR. TEDDY BEAR
> (to REAPER)
> I was thinking, maybe we're in the wrong business...

> REAPER
> Oh, I've had a very exciting life, just tired at the moment. If I hadn't laughed the first time I'd taken acid, I'd never have taken it again.

MR. TEDDY BEAR laughs, DRAC does not react, RUBY and CLOWN look around and make no visible comment, no change in their expressions.

> FADE TO BLACK

Scene 2:

A white room, slightly off balance, the decor is deteriorated haiku...nothing is symmetrical in the room. There are faint suggestions of gentle psychedelic decoration. The wire fences, steel factories and freeways, seen through the windows, project the feeling that all is as an El Greco painting. All is stark, bleak, bare, devoid of covering. Everything's in the open, with the laugh laughing at the laugh. Foghorns are heard in the distance.

RUBY is in bed, watching television disinterestedly. LADY CRYSTAL is on the floor, drawing. A boy of eighteen is bound and gagged in a corner of the room on the floor...we recognize him as CANDY. REAPER comes in angrily and lashes out at RUBY.

> REAPER
> Don't you get tired of watching television?

> RUBY
> (doesn't move, replies quietly)
> Nobody I know acts the way they do
> on television. It's all
> propaganda, some sort of
> insidious, suggestive new type of
> thought control. As though they
> were reinterpreting conventional
> ways of thinking, seeing, talking,
> being. I think it has to do with
> the destruction and re-education
> of habit formation processes.

REAPER plops down on the side of the bed and hugs RUBY.

                    REAPER
    Oh, baby, baby, I really love you
    so, but I'd never try to stop you
    if you ever wanted to go. After
    all, nothing's permanent, you
    know. We can always do it again.

                    RUBY
    Ohhhh, this is absurd.

                    REAPER
    I mean, oh, well, maybe not.
                 (shrugs)
    I must be getting old.

                    RUBY
    (shivers, looking abandoned)
    I suddenly feel so cold. People
    don't die from wishing, do they?
    I know it can happen the other
    way, all that energy.
    (reaches out and hugs REAPER)
        Baby, if I was sure you were
    straight, I'd make love to you
    every night.

REAPER looks at her, then looks away
speculatively. LADY CRYSTAL looks up from her
drawing, stares intensely at RUBY, as REAPER
rises and leaves quietly.

                 LADY CRYSTAL
    I was in a house of darkness, a
    deserted mansion. I'd been there
    before, all was darkness. There
    were noises from the front room.
    I ran to the door. First I saw
    shadows, then I saw the children,
    ragged, hippie children, who were
    as silhouettes. I flew above
    them. I wasn't going forward or
    backward. Then I woke up.

> RUBY
> (nods)
> He was jealous of me. I'd never
> met a boy who was jealous of me
> before.
> (gesticulates haphazardly)
> When he said I was just mad
> because my pants fit him better
> than they fit me, I should have
> said,
> (assumes another voice)
> "Well, you had to wait long
> enough for them."

RUBY looks beyond LADY CRYSTAL, then turns back
to her.

> RUBY
> But I didn't. But it's true, it's
> really true. He keeps me because
> he wants my pants, or whatever
> else I might have.
> (disgustedly)
> Too bad my boots don't fit
> him! Or my underwear!

LADY CRYSTAL laughs, going back to her drawing.

> RUBY
> Perhaps that's what comes from
> sharing the same outfit too much.

CANDY squirms in the corner. RUBY lifts up the
gag and sticks a candy bar in his mouth,
cautioning him to stop struggling and trying to
break free.

> RUBY
> While life lasted, we lived for
> others. Now, after death, we live
> for ourselves...

RUBY reaches under the bed, takes out a jewel
box and begins to fix by herself.

RUBY
But chemicals do take me halfway
there!

RUBY kneels on the floor in Japanese samurai
fashion and opens the jewel box, takes out a
spoon, wipes it with a cloth, puts a few grains
of crystal (white powder) into the spoon, adds a
few drops of distilled water, strikes a match,
heats up the spoon. She takes a plastic spike
in one hand, after tying off the top of her
forearm with a scarf, part of which she holds in
her teeth...while pumping up a vein with her
fist. When the vein is bulging under the skin,
she puts the hypodermic needle in the liquid of
dissolved methamphetamine and distilled water,
draws up the liquid in the spoon into the hypo,
and then, while holding the end of the scarf in
her teeth to keep the pressure on the vein,
sticks the needle into the vein and pushes the
liquid, while bringing back blood into the
needle and then pushing the top of the hypo down
to put the blood back into her arm.

She opens her fist and releases the tie in her
teeth, takes a deep breath, takes the hypo out
of her arm, squirting it into the spoon to make
sure it is empty. She adds distilled water to
the spoon, sucks the liquid back up into the
needle, and then into a cotton wad...for later.
Having cleaned the needle again, she puts the
items back into the jewel box, closes it, and
returns it to its hiding place.

                                FADE TO BLACK

                END ACT III

ACT IV

Scene 1:

Surreal atmosphere. Foghorns are faintly heard, or perhaps a saxophone. It is seven o'clock on a bleak Sunday morning. RUBY, wearing a dilapidated, torn corduroy coat, broken-heeled boots, carrying a six-pack of Coke bottles, is walking down a broken concrete city hill. Ahead of her, farther down the street, an elderly man and woman are waiting for a bus. The man is holding a paper sack. RUBY haphazardly kicks an empty orange juice bottle with her foot. There is a loud clanging noise. The elderly couple turns around, watching her.

> RUBY
> (hesitantly to other woman)
> Is that store open?

> OLD WOMAN
> (shakes her head)
> No.

> RUBY
> Ohhh.

> OLD WOMAN
> 7:30 on weekdays, but I don't
> think on Sundays...

RUBY looks in the store window. The proprietress inside shakes her head. RUBY continues down the hill. She walks slowly, following her reflection in the passing window panes, occasionally lingering on street corners. RUBY is as a child; while walking, she is talking to herself.

> RUBY
> We're running in a big race, a
> cross-country, obstacle-course
> marathon. The point is to make
> all the obstacles and come in
> first. Nobody's made all the
> obstacles yet. They've died
> instead. Someone will; it's only
> a matter of perfecting the
> technique, a contest in intensity.
> Who can do the most without
> copping out!
>   Like we're playing chicken
> and anything goes! It's a race to
> beat the devil at his own game.
> God's too tame...
>   So, where's the wonder? When
> nothing's bad any more, where's
> the motivation come from? Some of
> the children still believe in
> their fantasies. It's only a
> matter of time before they get
> used to them. I know a girl who
> wants to be a legend; she's
> halfway there.

LADY CRYSTAL, the candy queen, appears as in a
dream sequence. She is wearing a long hooded
cloak and little round glasses. Under the cloak
she wears a short, rainbow-striped dress and
over-knee boots. She is dancing, surrounded by
strobe lights and electronic music. As RUBY
continues down the sidewalk, this apparition
engulfs her. It's as though she were in the
street and an electric auditorium at the same
time, or that electric auditorium were in the
street.

> RUBY
> I know a girl who wants to be a
> legend; she's halfway there.
>   Lady Crystal, the candy
> queen, she wants people to
> recognize her name.

RUBY (cont.)
Lady Crystal, the candy queen, she
turns you on, inside and out, then
leaves before you find out what
it's all about.
Lady Crystal, the candy
queen, who made her first evil
vow, dancing on the grave of a
long-dead witch, when she was
fourteen...

RUBY stops at a corner, looks in her pockets,
takes out some change, counts it, shrugs her
shoulders, replaces the money and continues on
dejectedly.

RUBY
I've only one cigarette left, and
nineteen cents...
All motions must be graceful,
as though gestures made by dancers
in some ball, some absurd ballet.
(changes her walk into a dance)
Winter is almost here, sweet,
sad winter. The time of baptism
and hibernation. Winter...a
ragged, tattered, old-faced child
who's so very tired, yet knows not
how to rest, so stands against a
wall, begging with a golden bowl.
(looks around)
Welcome, winter, spirit of
forsaken fear.
(changes her tone again, thinking of REAPER)
I hardly ever go out with him
any more. I find the dying
children boring and depressing.
There's nothing to be done for
them, there's nothing to be done
for me.
We're all trying to kill
ourselves, to escape the pain of
having to see, of having to be...

RUBY turns down a garbage can-lined alley.
She's taking something out of her pockets. She
crouches down between two of the filthy, rusted
garbage cans to put her outfit together...she's
going to fix.

>   RUBY
> There was a girl, she pursued
> studies involving the relationship
> between spiritualism and
> philosophy. She was heavily into
> astrological and mathematical
> theories...all this is so
> familiar...

After RUBY shoots up, she passes out. REAPER
enters and finds her, wakes her up, brushes her
off, and walks her to the welfare office. She
obviously needs help.

>   FADE TO BLACK

Scene 2:

A room of chairs and magazine-covered tables.
RUBY and REAPER are two among the many young,
shabby, long-haired, pimply faced specimens of
deranged, chameleonistic disorientation sitting
in the room.

>   RUBY
>   (disgustedly, bewildered, to REAPER)
> The social revolution that's going
> on seems to be most apparent in
> the relief office.

REAPER grunts. RUBY becomes even more serious,
trying to catch REAPER's attention.

>   RUBY
> The doctor, Dr. Stewart, that I
> saw, was dressed for his part,
> that of a country doctor.

RUBY (cont.)
I guess he thought it would be
easier to relate to his patients
that way. He wouldn't give me any
vitamins. Said most Americans had
had too many vitamins anyway. He
was trying to psych me out. He
kept talking to me. I kept
saying, "Goodbye, doctor."
    I don't know why I didn't
want to talk to him. One of the
women, when I filled out the form,
took down the notation for rent
being fifty dollars. I wonder if
they'll give it to me?
    (dejectedly)
    I doubt it. And then Mother,
when she got my letter asking her
for money, she called the fuzz,
told them I was on drugs. God,
she could have sent me the money
she used on the phone. That's
maternal love!

REAPER
Why do you care?

REAPER gets up from his slouch, goes over to a
child's table covered with magazines and toys,
and begins to play Chinese checkers with himself
taking all four sides. One of the people on the
other side of the room is talking about the
weather; an old man with ragged clothes is
complaining about the two bucks he spent on the
taxi fare to get there; one of the other girls,
also ragged and sick, says that he should ask
the social worker to give it back to him.

RUBY
(looks out window)
The day is quite grey, there is a
faintly blue fog haze, earthquake
weather!

REAPER stops playing Chinese checkers, sits down by RUBY and beings to recite his favorite mantra, while waiting for his social worker.

> REAPER
> I am the devil, I am the devil, I am the devil. There is no sanity anywhere, there is no sanity anywhere, there is no sanity anywhere...

RUBY leans over and touches his arm, looking at him significantly, then towards the door, scratching her arm.

> RUBY
> C'mon, honey, let's go get jobs. No use hanging around here in this ambulatory cemetery...

> REAPER
> I was wondering when you were going to come to that conclusion, my sweet!

He stands up, gallantly extends his arm, which RUBY takes, and they glide towards the door, opening it carefully, and slip out.

FADE TO BLACK

Scene 3:

Leaving the dismal relief office, REAPER and RUBY float along the sidewalk lined with anonymous-looking office buildings. RUBY has her head down, her hands in her pockets. She's looking for money on the ground, and thinking about how she's going to get straight again. Her previous shot is beginning to wear off; coming down is such a drag.

REAPER is going through the money he has in his pocket in his mind, while thinking about how

he's going to ditch the broad, get his shot, and
then maybe find her again.

A coffee shop known as The Hot Dog Palace is at
the end of the block they're walking along. The
place is large, with big plate-glass windows,
white tables, sterile white walls, a jukebox and
a glass counter, behind which is the COUNTERMAN,
with a white cap on his head. There are
assorted pastries, donuts, cookies, behind the
counter on display. There is also a coffee
machine with four glass coffee pots at various
levels of full. Next to that is the cash
register. The COUNTERMAN wipes cups with his
rag and watches as RUBY and REAPER take seats.

> RUBY
> You gotta help me out. You can't
> just leave me here. Hey, can I
> play the music box? What do you
> want me to play, honey? Maybe I
> could get another job dancing.
> That's what I'll do! You get us
> some stuff, we'll go somewhere to
> get straight, then I'll make the
> rounds. Next time, it'll be my
> treat, okay? What do you say?

> REAPER
> Look, baby, I'll get you some
> coffee and here's some change for
> the box. Then I'm gonna go out
> that door. You're gonna stay here
> 'til I get back. I don't know how
> long that'll be. I gotta go a few
> places. It might take an hour, it
> might be all night. Lucky this is
> a twenty-four hour place.

REAPER gets the coffee from the COUNTERMAN and
comes back to the table, giving it to RUBY. He
pulls some pills from his pocket and gives them
to RUBY, who looks at them, then at him.

               RUBY
     What're these for?

               REAPER
     These'll hold you for a few hours.
     They're black beauties. Sip the
     coffee straight and black, get
     into the sounds, keep your mouth
     shut, and just hang out.

               RUBY
     (reaches hesitantly for the pills)
     Okay, honey. I'll just hang out.
     You got any paper and a pen?
     Maybe I'll write a few sketches,
     draw a few poems...I'll design my
     next costume, plan my new act.
     There's another club, a new one
     just opened up on Broadway. Heard
     they might need a dancer.

               REAPER
     (rising from the table)
     Okay, sweetie, that's the chick.
     Catch you later, stay cool.

REAPER reaches into his jacket and gives her a
tattered steno pad and a pen.

               REAPER
     Here you go.

RUBY looks up at him, motions for him to come
closer so she can whisper in his ear.

               RUBY
     You be cool, baby. You don't
     leave me here all night.
     (kisses him lightly on the lips)
          We have fun, don't we, hon?

               REAPER
     (pulls away after accepting the kiss)
     Gotta go, babe. See you later.

As he bops out the door, RUBY puts one of the black beauties in her mouth, takes a sip of coffee, counts the change on the table, takes a coin, gets up from the table, walks slowly toward the jukebox, puts the coin in the machine, and reads the selections. There are over a hundred listings, so she reads them while waiting for the pill to take effect.

After reading every selection, RUBY presses in six choices. The COUNTERMAN lights a cigarette and looks out the window as twilight descends on the city. Outside the window, cars go by, commuters returning home, a cop walks by on the evening patrol. Gentle jazz comes out of the jukebox as RUBY returns to her seat and gazes out the window, also wondering what the night will bring. She takes a sip of her coffee, picks up the pencil and begins to write.

> JUKEBOX
> Lost in the night... Out of
> sight... Neon lights... Shine so
> bright...
> Summer heat warms my sight...
> Winter snow turns into gold...
> White rock rises... As the ice
> grows cold...
> The ice grows cold... Speed
> your love back to me... My body's
> sizzling for all to see... My
> mind's burning with your memory...
> Speed your love back to me...
> Lost in the night... Out of
> sight... Neon lights... Shine so
> bright...
> Speed your love back to me...
> Back to me...

The words sound sultry, while the saxophone, bass guitar, and piano play in the background. RUBY looks up from her paper, reads it back to herself quietly, moving her lips, whispering the words. A couple of street kids come into the place. A BOY of seventeen dressed in black

jeans, black leather jacket, black hair, black
motorcycle boots. His GIRL companion has long,
straight blonde hair, black tights, purple-and-
black skirt with purple blouse, soft black
shoes. They stand in front of the glass counter
looking at the pastries and cookies, softly
discussing what they want. The COUNTERMAN looks
at them, putting his cigarette into an ashtray
by the cash register.

                    BOY
          Couple of glazed donuts and
          coffees.

COUNTERMAN nods, pours coffee into paper cups,
puts donuts onto napkins.

                    COUNTERMAN
          Two dollars.

The BOY opens his wallet, takes out two crisp
bills and hands them to the COUNTERMAN. The
GIRL picks up her coffee and donut and leads the
way to one of the tables by the window as the
BOY puts his wallet back in his pocket, picks up
his coffee and donut and follows her. They put
down their food and sit down, staring at each
other and out the window at the night as the
jukebox plays another tune.

                    JUKEBOX
          First time I saw you, baby, I knew
          that you were mine. Then I saw
          you on the corner, looking so
          pretty and fine...
               Later, when I saw you walking
          through the city, thought you
          might be looking for company...
               Then I saw you in the park,
          hanging out with everybody...
               Oh, babe, when you gonna come
          on home with me? Oh, babe, I see
          you goin' 'round with so many...

                    JUKEBOX (cont.)
Babe, babe, when you gonna come
home with me... And be mine...
We could be so happy... We could
live so fine...
        Oh, babe, ain't gonna ask you
but one more time. Come on home
now, come on home and be mine...
We could live so fine...

As words die out, instrumental melody line comes
through again...and another sound is faintly
heard...that of a wooden recorder...then, in the
door of The Hot Dog Palace comes a GIRL of
seventeen. She's putting a wooden recorder into
the pocket of her green army parka, while
walking over to the glass counter and looking at
the supply of assorted pastries. The COUNTERMAN
has his back to her, staring out the window.

                    GIRL
        Black coffee, please.

The COUNTERMAN turns and gets her coffee. The
GIRL fumbles in her pocket and gives him a
dollar and he gives her fifty cents change. She
reaches out for the cup, takes it...nods her
head as thanks, turns slowly around to survey
the room, moves toward the round table in the
middle of the floor between the jukebox and the
couple sitting at the window. She puts the
coffee cup on the table and jumps up on the
stool in front of it. She adjusts her parka,
takes a sip of her coffee, takes out her change,
counts it, gets up, goes over to the jukebox,
puts a couple of coins in the machine, and
proceeds to read the selections as RUBY did.
After a few minutes of this, the GIRL presses
several buttons several times, then returns to
her stool in front of the round table with a
pole through the middle of it, and takes another
sip of her coffee. She then looks at RUBY
sitting at her table gazing into the air, turns

and looks at the couple sitting by the window, then turns and looks at the COUNTERMAN.

As the new song begins to play on the jukebox, the GIRL takes a bottle of soap bubble liquid out of her parka pocket and is blowing soap bubbles into the air as, outside, the light brightens into a misty mist of foggy dew-drenched San Francisco sunrise...and the stage becomes a surreal dream scene of rainbow-tinted soap bubbles floating in the air, all around the people hanging out at the tables and behind the counter.

> JUKEBOX--A GIRL'S VOICE
> Colors, colors, colors in the air.
> Colors, colors, colors
> everywhere...
> Red, yellow, blue and green.
> Black, white, brown and tan...
> So many colors, colors in the
> air, so many colors, colors
> everywhere...
> Purple, lavender, magenta,
> chartreuse, silver, gold,
> turquoise, jade and amber hue...
> Colors, colors, colors in the
> air. Colors, colors, colors
> everywhere...
> So many colors, colors in the
> air, so many colors, colors
> everywhere...
> Red, yellow, blue and green,
> gray, black, white, brown and tan,
> burgundy, orange, purple, too...
> Lavender, magenta,
> chartreuse, silver, gold,
> turquoise, jade and amber hues...
> Colors, colors, colors in the
> air. Colors, colors, colors
> everywhere...

JUKEBOX--A GIRL'S VOICE (cont.)
So many colors, colors in the air.
So many colors, colors
everywhere...

As the words fade, the GIRL in the army-green
parka blows the bubbles into the air. As the
light of the rising sun illuminates the room,
all is as a tableau...the house lights dim and
the characters are seen sitting at the tables in
silhouette as once again the sad refrain of the
"Colors" song plays in the background.

REAPER appears in the doorway of the restaurant,
looking beat from hours spent dodging the heat
on the streets. From the jukebox, a trumpet is
heard playing a melancholy riff in the
background. REAPER shambles into The Hot Dog
Palace. RUBY's been waiting for him all night.
She looks at him as he comes over and sits down
beside her, nudging her with his arm. The
trumpet plays in the distance as he whispers.

REAPER
I seen the dealer, and I copped a
score. He was hanging on the
corner in front of the store...

RUBY shakes her head, runs her finger up and
down the outside of the coffee mug resting on
the table, shrugging her shoulders as if cold.
She's been sitting there all night, waiting, and
now she can't wait any more. But she has to
contain her impatience or REAPER won't treat her
any better than any other "runaway chore."

RUBY
(running her hands through her hair)
Getting high on the rush, like
never before...

REAPER
People were standing in line...

                    RUBY
          Wanting more?

The trumpet plays in the background, the same
riff as earlier, only slower and longer...like
neon fading into the dawn's early morning light.

REAPER acts as though wired, with short, jerky
movements, opening and closing his hand in front
of RUBY, indicating he's got something to share
with her, wondering if she'd like to split or is
she still lost in her personal daydream...

                    REAPER
          (repeating softly in her ear)
          I seen the dealer, and I copped a
          score.

                    RUBY
              (nods, whispers)
          Now you getting high off the rush,
          like never before...

                    REAPER
          Yeah, he was hanging on the corner
          in front of the store, dialing
          numbers on the phone to bring down
          the man, hiding in the line,
          people going 'round the street,
          ain't no one there looking so beat
          as the dealer when he's on the
          trail of the heat...

                    RUBY
           (turning to look at REAPER)
          You mean he was tracking down the
          man, trying to discover the leak
          in the frying pan?

                    REAPER
                  (chuckling)
Yeah, you might put it like that.
So many busted, so many dead,
makes us think there's somebody
inside sprinkling us with
lead...somebody working two jobs
at the same time. When we find
him, won't be no time to say
goodbye.

At this last pronouncement, REAPER gets up from
the table, floating away, out the door, into the
early morning dawn of another day once more.

                     RUBY
(humming softly to herself while writing)
          Seen the dealer and I copped a
          score, he was coming out of the
          candy store, with a big stack of
          books, and bills, like never
          before...yeah...
               He was wasted and beat, this
          cat from the street, with the look
          of a fugitive, running from the
          heat... He said, when I asked him
          if he had any hid, he said no, no,
          anything but that...

As the lights come down, RUBY continues singing
to herself while writing in The Hot Dog Palace,
in this early morning dream...

                     RUBY
          He said, you wanna go to dinner,
          you wanna see a show...that's what
          he said. When I asked him for a
          touch, he gave me such a rush, I
          felt his tingling in my head.
               I was electrified, couldn't
          decide what to do instead, yeah,
          he went right to my head...

Lights continue to go down on RUBY and come up
on the silhouette of REAPER, snapping fingers,
cool cat prance step, streamlined zoot-suit
presence turned into a midnight stroller
lounging through the electric night, as might a
prowler through a lair, as might a melody
through a horn, a mellow alto saxophone...

RUBY sings her words to herself while adding
commas or insertions with the pencil as REAPER
continues dancing his shadowy ballet,
silhouetted in the foggy haze of early dawn's
gaze...

                    RUBY
          In and out of shadows, like a
          light he goes, a neon Charlie
          Chaplin coming down, doing the
          town, tripping all up and down the
          underground... Ruby's at the
          Palace, he can feel her heat, he
          can't just leave her stranded,
          strung out like a beat... He's
          got to give her something to hold
          her nice and neat...
             It's that kind of thing, the
          starkness of the dream, the
          blindness of the bare reality a
          hard hype knows, it's hard to
          overcome, it seems...like the neon
          whiteness of a crystal mind,
          waiting in The Hot Dog Palace,
          where everyone's hanging on
          time...
             Remembering the blue
          daydreams, waiting for the
          medicine that'll keep away the
          screams of pain and persecution
          felt when the daylight streams in
          through the windows as the crowds
          begin to mingle with the outside
          scene...

>   RUBY (cont.)
> Like an all-night automat on
> Forty-second Street, or elsewhere
> on Times Square, it's a brutal
> nightmare, this scream of pain
> heard when fantasy's a scheme of
> innocence and reality's illegal
> dependence... Where is that man
> that left me here? Where is that
> mother Reaper, he could be
> anywhere!

RUBY runs her fingers through her hair, tosses
her head, trying to get the monkey out of
there...picks up some change and, after counting
it, plays the jukebox as the lights...

>   ...FADE TO BLACK

Scene 4:

Later that evening. The lights come up on the
sidewalk in front of The Hot Dog Palace. We see
two figures sitting under a tree bordering the
sidewalk. One of the figures is playing a steel
drum while intoning "Ommmmmmmmmm." The tones are
sounding deep and resonant. The other figure is
playing a silver flute, complementing the notes
of the steel drum. Passing people occasionally
drop money into a hat placed in front of the
steel drum. There is a third person playing the
tambourine and singing the words of the song,
"Where Did Those Years Go?" as the flute and the
drum person play the notes of the same tune.
The flute player is the girl in the army-green
parka. Two other MUSICIANS play nearby.

>   STEEL DRUM PLAYER
> Ohmmm...alms...ohmmm...alms...
> Ohmmm...alms...ohmmm...alms...

                    GIRL
                  (singing)
Leaves blowing along the sidewalk,
sky blue and white above. Leaves
blowing along the sidewalk, when I
done found my love. It was a
winter's evening many years ago.
We'd been walking in the city that
we loved so...Leaves blowing along
the sidewalk, sky blue and white
above.

        How the memories do flood my
mind with images of events of long
ago. It seems just like
yesterday... Where did those
years go?

As the GIRL stops singing, the flute player
plays the tune again as the steel drum
improvises in the background. The player has
stopped the "ohmmm...alms" chant to concentrate
on his playing, as a crowd has gathered around
the trio, listening to the song and the sounds
of these street players...the flute, the drum
and the tambourine.

Eventually the song ends, the crowd drifts away,
and the street musicians decide to get coffee.
They pack up their instruments, wander down the
sidewalk, cross the street and go into the Caffe
Trieste, a neighborhood bar across the street
from City Lights Bookstore. Finding an empty
table in the back, they arrange themselves and
then, as one goes to the bar to order espressos
and another goes to the jukebox to play
quarters, the GIRL looks at her watch and, as
the music comes on, she turns to go.

                STEEL DRUM PLAYER
          A domani! (See you tomorrow!)

The GIRL nods her head and hops out into the
night as the espresso arrives at the table.

TAMBOURINE PLAYER
Dobbiamo accelerare il passo! Ti
accomodero io! (We must hasten!
I'll fix you up!)

STEEL DRUM PLAYER
Mi accontento facilmente. (I'm
easily pleased.)

MUSICIAN 1
D'inverno le giornate si
accorciano. (In winter the days
become shorter.)

TAMBOURINE PLAYER
Ho Furia. Devo accudire alle mie
faccende. (I'm in a hurry. I
must attend to my duties.)

STEEL DRUM PLAYER
Siamo appena giunti. (We have
just arrived.)

MUSICIAN 1
Prestar giuramento? (To take an
oath?)

TAMBOURINE PLAYER
Venir meno ad un giuramento. (To
break an oath.)

STEEL DRUM PLAYER
I ragazzi, in casa... (The boys
at home...)

TAMBOURINE PLAYER
Si lasci guidare da me. Una per
di gusto! (Allow me to guide you.
A person of good taste.)

MUSICIAN 1
Che cosa intende dire? (What do
you mean?)

STEEL DRUM PLAYER
Cerchiami di intenderei. (Let's
try to understand each other.)

MUSICIAN 1
Mia Cara amica, ha un carattere
docile. (My friend, he has a mild
disposition.)

TAMBOURINE PLAYER
Caschi il mondo, cedo le armi,
celebrare...un libro come il mio.
(Come what may, I surrender to
celebrate...a book like mine.)

MUSICIAN 1
(to STEEL DRUM PLAYER)
Come triste! (How sad it is!)

STEEL DRUM PLAYER
Come mi vide, mi venna incontro.
(As soon as he saw me, he came
towards me.)

MUSICIAN 1
Sento dei colpi alla porta.
Arrivare in cima alla montagna.
(I hear a knocking at the door.
To reach the top of the mountain.)

MUSICIAN 2
Cio non importa. Tuttocio mi
preoccupa. La ferita si sta
cicatrizzando. (It doesn't
matter. All this worries me. The
wound is healing.)

STEEL DRUM PLAYER
A chi tutto, a chi niente. Ci
Comprendiamo! (Some have too
much, some have too little. We
understand each other!)

TAMBOURINE PLAYER
Cara meo bambino, cara meo mon
amour, cara meo con brio, ti
accomodero io...once more...

Lights of the night come on as the late night
show crowds from Finocchio's begin to crowd the
street, pouring out of the theater, mingling on
the sidewalk with the waste and beat...the neon
blinks, and...

FADE TO BLACK

END ACT IV

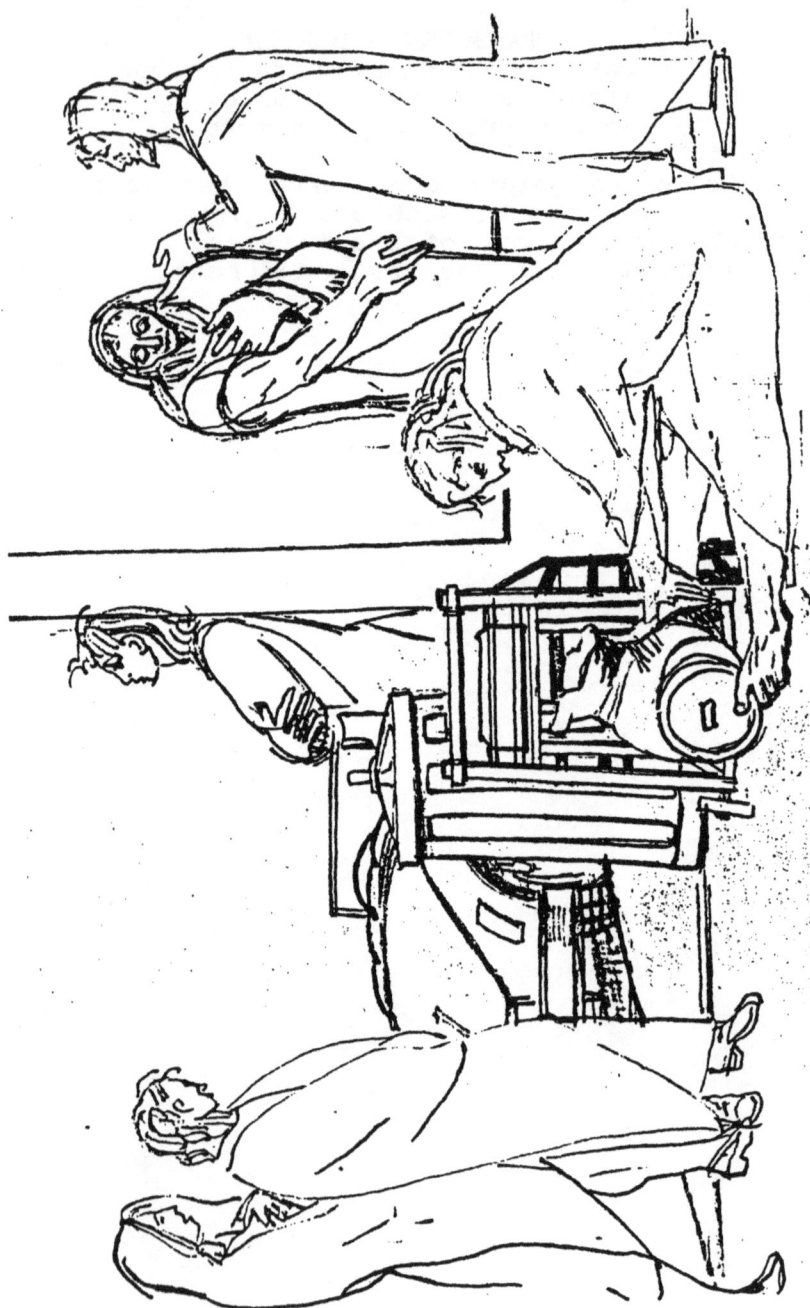

EPILOGUE

Fog-misted morning-grey light. The GIRL comes
back in a daze. She's singing to herself as she
walks lightly, weaving through the surrounding
haze. Hanging out in front of the Caffe
Trieste, she makes up a song as she looks
through the windows.

> GIRL
> Hey, hey daddy, hey, hey daddio,
> been gone a long-gone train,
> coming on in through the rain,
> long-gone train, coming back to
> you again...been a long-gone
> train, longtime overdue...On the
> tracks of my tears, I've rolled
> through the years, tripping away
> all my fears...
> Hey, hey daddy, hey, hey
> daddio, this rocking horse is
> rolling, coming on back to you,
> like a long-time train, way long
> overdue...

Emerging from the shadows of the alley across
the way, next to City Lights Bookstore, Daddy
emerges...he is the STEEL DRUM PLAYER. He steps
up to the girl, walking in a way reminiscent of
a vaudeville comedian, like a sad clown turned
into a Chaplinesque mime. With his finger in
the "shhhh" sign against his lips, he comes up
to her and puts his arm around her to warm her.

> STEEL DRUM PLAYER
> Cool it, kid! Tighten up the lid!
> Keep it well hid, protect all the
> secrets that you know.

STEEL DRUM PLAYER (cont.)
Don't blow the show...if you give
anything away, how you gonna have
the money to pay the man when he
come knocking on your door? Hey,
yeah, that's the way it is, now
you know! Just like Lady Day, you
got some strange fruit to sing
about today...the prisons are
packed with your brothers...now
this I know you know...some people
think your generation's just
another token payroll...

A GUY going into the bookstore stops and sees
the couple across the street in front of the
Caffe Trieste. He starts rapping and doesn't go
into the bookstore. Instead, he sits down in
front of the bookstore display window on the
sidewalk, pulls a notebook from his pocket and
starts talking as he's writing, bopping his feet
in time to the beat.

GUY
Across all the obscene boundaries
of time, place, space...he went to
Albany, New York to rock the
cradle and signify the face...he
read love songs, funny songs and
sad songs...to the "kids" as he
rocked the cradle, of the crib,
through the maze of labyrinthian
haze...in the valley of the gun--
hidden well from the sun--across
all the obscene boundaries, he did
run...

GUY 2 emerges from the bookstore, sees GUY
sitting there with notebook in his hand, pencil
poised on the paper and begins rapping.

                    GUY 2
          Yeah, wow! The Cat climbed down
          from the tree and he jumped into a
          crib for all to see, and he sang
          us some sweet melodies...

                    GUY
          (looking up from his writing)
          Everybody stood up and applauded
          sweetly, cause the cat was a beat,
          with a beard, yeah, he said he
          isn't but we know he is cause he
          looks wasted from the heat, like
          an outlaw on the run, searching
          for cover under the sun, he
          covered my life with a drawing
          that was better than any
          gun...yeah...

STEEL DRUM PLAYER puts his hand under GIRL's
chin. As he lifts her face, he brushes away her
tears.

                    STEEL DRUM PLAYER
          Perche fare piancere? (Why do you
          cry?)

                    GIRL
          (pulls her face away defiantly)
          Il via io ridere. (That's the way
          I laugh.)

As they talk, the light changes, other PEOPLE
start appearing on the sidewalk, the day is
getting under way. GIRL and STEEL DRUM PLAYER
walk together, singing...

GIRL & STEEL DRUM PLAYER
Civediamo domaini mattina, cara
meo, bambino, mon amour... (See
you tomorrow morning, dearest
baby, my love...)

FADE TO BLACK

END EPILOGUE

FINIS

STREET KIDS,

or,
LES ENFANTS SANS MAISONS

A LIBRETTO OF FOLK OPERA ABOUT INNER CITY URBAN LIFE

Ruby and Reaper have been together for quite some time now, and their world has grown even smaller than when we last saw them, except for the addition of a young child. The once-active dancer/singer/writer now has only one ruling passion, and no matter what the other street kids say or do, she will complete her destiny as will the others, including Reaper, her old man. Set against the backdrop of inner-city unrest, the in-depth view of subterranean existence and its consequences is filled with cameos of the children of this plane and their thoughts on where they've been...and where they're going.

concentrating on the meaning of existence, visualizing
anticipated happenings and expectations before returning to
their bodies once again, the vehicle used for participa-
tion in the lives of men...

and
the voice in my head says did you learn those things in
school?
yeah!

a long time ago, in the 1950s 'round the time of billie
and charlie, there were soundings by allen and mccarthy...
one talking singing rhymes and promoting mimes...the
other calling people names, accusing them of crimes...

CAST:

THE SHADES	Street gang
MERK	Leader of the gang
ANGEL	A shadowy spirit
CHARON (CHERRY)	A cabbie
RUBY	A young woman in a ragged red dress
EBONY	RUBY's son, a child of five or six
REAPER	RUBY's husband, an old man, who could be EBONY's father
GUARD	An anonymous character with a white mask for a face
JUNKIE	A girl of indeterminate age
VOICE	

SETS:

Act 1, Scene 1	Styx Alley
Act 1, Scene 2	Styx Alley
Act 2	Rooftop above Styx Alley
Act 3, Scene 1	Sidewalk in Skid Row District of City
Act 3, Scene 2	Inside Tenement Apartment
Act 3, Scene 3	A Cell Block in State Penitentiary

PROLOGUE

The melody of the song "In This Lifetime" plays on the piano offstage, sounding as though it is coming from the bar off Styx Alley. The colors of midnight in the underworld on the outskirts of town, or the Skid Row of a major city, silhouette the misty backdrop of tenements outlined in the distance, in back of the crossroads that lead to the entrance of Styx Alley.

Styx Alley is the hangout of MERK and THE SHADES--a street gang that refers to the buildings as Hades. They are made up as mimes to enhance the flavor of the piece.

* * * * *

"In This Lifetime"

Night time, neon light time, makes me wanna get so high, in the night time...

Shadow show time, how the week does fly. Weekend night, stoned time, it's time to get high...

In the night time, street life time, everybody's got a line, everybody's looking for a dime, in their own way...

Night time, neon light time, makes me wanna get so high, in this life time...

* * * * *

As the words fade, the piano continues on to play "The Purple Hood Suite" of which this song is the introduction. "The Purple Hood Suite" sounds in various forms throughout.

ACT I

Scene 1:

Night. MERK and THE SHADES are hanging out in Styx Alley, casing the shadows floating towards CHERRY, just up the street from Tenement Valley (which everyone knows as Hades), set on the outskirts of the big city, where the freak dog with three heads and a dragon tail stands as sentinel howling at the moon, sounding like a voice from a tomb.

Whenever the gang hears the dog howl, they know something is up. Towards the alley comes RUBY running madly, hair streaming wildly, red ribbon waving in the wind. The tattered, ragged dress she wears is covered with blood. Right behind her, with a tambourine, is EBONY. REAPER chases them into the alley. Out in the street, sounds of screaming and rioting start coming from the tenements. MERK turns to THE SHADES, fading into the purple silhouettes of late-night space light.

MERK
Hades sure is hot tonight!

SHADES
(chorus)

Yeah!

                    MERK
        Looks like there's another riot
        going down, all around, yeah,
        there's another riot going down,
        all around, yeah, there's another
        rumble gonna happen in the
        underground.

                    SHADES
(ghostly chorus in folk rock-and-roll sing-song)
        Yeah, whenever Ruby come running
        with her kid and Reaper a chasing
        after 'em, like that, you know
        something's gonna happen,
        something's gonna happen in the
        town. Hades gonna swing with war,
        all through the underground.

                    MERK
        Yeah, something terrible gonna be
        coming down out there, just on the
        outskirts of town.

                    SHADES
        When Hades get hot, all souls
        gonna rot, whether they like it or
        not. Yeah, when Hades get hot,
        all souls gonna rot, when Hades
        get hot.

                    ANGEL
        Say, what you say, Man?

Sound effects for crowd scene. THE SHADES turn
around to look at ANGEL, from the underground,
standing fast with a gun in his hand, pointing
the piece at MERK. The sounds of the night fall
all around as the stream of looters are heard,
running fast, busting out of Tenement Valley.
Their shadows holding bottles of liquor are
sometimes reflected on the walls of the alley.
The guys in Styx Alley know what's up. Lady
RUBY and her kid EBONY are cornered by REAPER
once more. While the ANGEL of Change holds up

THE SHADES, the Misery Mob races by, heading for the city. Heading for the man's mainline with liquor on the brain. Tenement Valley screams with pain as the riot begins, and the flames shoot higher; there is smoke everywhere. The souls are trashing Hades. Tired of the poverty, the stagnation, disease, sick of the insanity, cruelty, brutality, they see every day, everywhere in Tenement Valley. The souls are tearing down the house of pain, they are breaking away from the ghetto. They pour out onto the street, with the starlight so neat, out on the street, with the wind and the rain. They stream out onto the street where they can feel again. MERK watches the action, wondering if he can do anything to help their souls with their reincarnation.

The sound of night drums sings in the distance as the crack of shattering glass falls through the night. Then a voice cries out in hideous delight.

> VOICE (O.S.)
> AIIIIIIIIII! HEEEEEEEEEEEEEE!
> AHHHHHHHHHH! AIIIIIIIIIIIIIIIII!

ANGEL puts down his gun and leans against the wall of the alley, looking at the gang of SHADES and their leader MERK, and at the girl RUBY, her kid EBONY and REAPER. ANGEL pulls a cigarette from a pack in the pocket in his t-shirt, puts it in his mouth, lights it with a cigarette lighter, then, with an arrogant air and a strut in his stride, circles the space in the middle of the alley.

> ANGEL
> (singing "Jail House Blues")
> Jail House Blues, Jail House
> Blues. From the top of my head,
> to the soles of my shoes, living
> with the Jail House Blues

                    ANGEL (cont.)
Been inside for six years now,
been inside so long, just decided
to make up a song...
      Looking out through steel
bars, grey skies is all I see,
with the Jail House Blues for
company...
      Jail House Blues all around
me...
      Ain't never any end to paying
dues, when you living with the
Jail House Blues
(looks around, saunters back to his gun)

                    SHADES
Amen, Man. Aaaaaamennnnn, Man!

                    MERK
Yeah, Man, we know where you
coming from, we know what you
mean, we all been locked up, some
of us still doing time, some of us
just hanging out, waiting for a
dime...you know what I mean?

ANGEL nods.

THE SHADES in Styx Alley hang out all night,
smoking and rapping 'bout the riot. The kid
EBONY falls asleep near his mother RUBY, who
curls up next to REAPER in a space along one
side of the alley wall. As the sun rises, the
Ashes remain, to remind everyone of the night-
time of pain. Tenement Valley had burned to the
ground. Hades had to change its name, until the
time for it to be again came. MERK, THE SHADES,
ANGEL, RUBY, EBONY, and REAPER survey the
remains while stretching, scratching, rubbing
sleep out of tired eyes. Cans of beer and soda
are passed around, and then we hear RUBY's
voice.

                    RUBY
                 (to REAPER)
Oh, Man, oh, Man, if you hadn't
gone off and left me that time,
everything would have been okay!

                    REAPER
Baby, how can you say that, I
didn't stick the spike in your
arm!

                    RUBY
Oh, Man, but you didn't stop it
either!

RUBY gets up, settles EBONY next to REAPER.

                    RUBY
             (singing "Nodding Out")
Walking down the street, feeling
so forlorn, remembering how you
were, on that other early morn...
        We'd been drinking burgundy
for many a day, yeah, we'd been
sharing a bottle to keep the blues
away...
        Then you went to the
hospital, and I was on my own,
with nothing but a needle and a
dealer to call home...
        Nothing but a needle and a
dealer to call home.
        Looking at the sky, and the
glass upon the ground, watching
the wind dance the ashes all
around, yeah, watching the wind
dance the ashes all around.
        There's glass on the ground,
Man, glass all over the ground...

                        REAPER
(gets up, puts his arm around RUBY's shoulder)
            C'mon, hon', let's forget about
            that, don't make no difference how
            you got the hype...don't make no
            matter, all that went before. I
            know you need your morning, so
            we'll just go looking for a dime
            once more...okay, Babe...

MERK and THE SHADES move closer. MERK nods his
head and starts talking to the sky. ANGEL and
THE SHADES know he's high. MERK's rapping to
RUBY and REAPER.

                        MERK
            It makes us cry to see our old
            friends die. Yeah, it makes us
            cry to see our old friends die
            from sticking needles in their
            arms to get high...
                We used to fly, miles up in
            the sky... Riding higher than the
            clouds, everybody was high, riding
            through the sky...
                The clouds drifted by... The
            trips we'd take, in the sky...
            (singing "We Flew Into the Sun")
                We flew into the sun, we
            transcended time, becoming ghostly
            people. Some thought death our
            only design, as Oriental myths
            changed the outlines of our lives
                (song ends; speaking now)
                We were looking for a space.
            We found a place; while becoming
            we found the rhyme... Psychedelia
            is dead. What remains, what
            remains?
            (turns to RUBY, looks directly at her)
                The Ashes remain, only the
            Ashes remain, Ashes and dust and
            rust...that's what remains, ashes
            and dust...and rust.

THE SHADES, REAPER, ANGEL, RUBY, and MERK know the feeling well. They nod and sigh, remembering all those highs. They dance, making fun of the memory, and sing.

> MERK & RUBY
> We flew into the sun, we
> transcended time...becoming
> ghostly people. Some thought
> death our only design...

> REAPER, ANGEL & THE SHADES
> As Oriental myths changed the
> outlines of our lives...
>   We were looking for a
> space...we found a place, while
> becoming we found the rhyme...

> FADE TO BLACK

Scene 2:

A few hours later...ANGEL talks to RUBY, while REAPER looks at her arm, tenderly touching it with his fingers. EBONY sits quietly chewing on a rag. MERK and THE SHADES are a few feet down the Alley polishing ANGEL's gun. They've taken it apart, and are cleaning each part before putting it back together again.

> ANGEL
> (to RUBY)
> You know what it means to be
> locked up, girl? You ever been
> searched physically in a shower,
> thrown into a jail cell, with
> nothing but a toilet, four walls,
> a ceiling, a locked door, and a
> cot for company?
>   Maybe one of the walls got a
> two-way mirror, and you know
> they're watching you and seeing
> anything you might do.

ANGEL (cont.)
What do you do, sitting there in
solitary isolation? Maybe you
cry, maybe you wish you could die.
Maybe there's holes in the panels
on the wall and on the ceiling.
Maybe you can try to count 'em,
maybe you fall asleep. Then,
maybe later, you locked up in
another place, with a bunch of
other weird people. There ain't
nothing to do but smoke and think.
Nothing to do but play Scrabble
and look out the window, or watch
the guards give shots and pills to
people. And nobody has anything
to do but sit around and talk, and
wait, and walk, and pace, and
wait...while thinking...and
looking for cigarettes, and
waiting, and walking, and
thinking, and talking, and pacing.
      And maybe one of the other
prisoners gets strapped to their
chair, and maybe another of the
prisoners tells horror stories of
what's happening on the other
wards...and there ain't nothing to
do but wait and walk, back and
forth, and wish there was some way
to get out, some way to get away,
some way to be free again...
      Some way to be alive again,
instead of just a number in a
book, a statistic in an almanac, a
case in a file in a cabinet, or
just another report on someone's
desk!

RUBY looks up at ANGEL, rubs her eyes with her
palms, and runs her fingers through her hair.

> RUBY
> Enough, Man, alright? You're
> giving me a headache with your
> lecture!

EBONY walks over to RUBY with his rag dragging
behind him, puts his hand on her arm, snuggling
his body against hers.

> EBONY
> Momma, I'm hungry...

> RUBY
> (hugs EBONY)
> Alright, Honey. We'll find
> something soon. Just be quiet and
> try to take another nap. Momma's
> busy now.

MERK looks toward RUBY, then saunters over and
kneels down beside her.

> MERK
> You gotta help yourself if you
> wanna make it today, you gotta
> help yourself, some say,
>   Help yourself, yeah, we gotta
> learn to help ourselves, we all
> gotta help ourselves today...

RUBY looks at MERK, still hugging EBONY, with
REAPER standing nearby.

> RUBY
> Yeah, went to see the doctor,
> everybody knows, doctor say, hey,
> Babe, what's the matter with your
> nose...it's a' running, you're a'
> sniffling as though you had a bad
> cold. Ain't that right, Reaper?

                    REAPER
          (nods; continues story)
          Yeah, that doctor told her,
          pneumonia, that doctor told her,
          you're shaking like you've really
          got a super cold.
          (looks at RUBY's face, arm around her)
                    Yeah, Babe, you really got a
          super cold...
          (puts hand on RUBY's forehead tenderly)
                    Yeah, Momma's little babe
          needs a short, a shot that's not
          too hot, just a little
          shot...yeah, Momma's babe needs a
          shot to get off...

REAPER looks at MERK, who is still standing by,
watching the condition of RUBY, who is holding
on to EBONY, who's fallen asleep again, with his
rag in his little baby hand. MERK turns and
walks back to THE SHADES lounging against a
wall.

                    MERK
          Everybody knows, everybody shows,
          even the sky knows, there's UFOs
          everywhere, taking off in the air.
          See the bright lights shining
          through the night. Orange suns
          big in the sky, orange suns travel
          high, in the sky.

As MERK gazes into the sky, ANGEL leaves his
place by EBONY, RUBY, and REAPER and, going over
to MERK, nudges him with his shoulder. Soft
piano music of "The Purple Hood Suite" plays in
the background.

                    ANGEL
          Remember the radicals, the
          crazies, the freaks and burlie
          shows, the serious beats?

> ANGEL (cont.)
> Remember the skyscrapers, how high
> they used to rise, up into the
> sky?

> MERK
> Yeah. We were the children below
> the city, wandering around hungry,
> our parents were dying from hot
> shots and blown out minds...We
> cried 'cause we didn't know what
> to do. Ain't nobody got the
> answers today, 'bout where the
> poor, hungry, tired, wasted people
> left over from the wars can stay.
> Ain't nobody got those kind of
> answers today, 'bout where the
> shadows and shades of yesterday
> can fade away.

ANGEL turns to THE SHADES, does a little dance
step, gesturing with his hands.

> ANGEL
> We play music to stay high, making
> music takes us into the sky.

> MERK
> (joins in, also dances around)
> Our souls fly as the rings of
> Saturn flash by. We used to play
> for nickels and dimes, now we play
> to get high!

> ANGEL & MERK
> Now we play to the sky, now we
> play to get high...

As ANGEL and MERK and THE SHADES dance around
chanting the words, the rain begins to fall...

ANGEL, MERK & THE SHADES
We play music to stay high, making
music takes us into the sky, our
souls fly as the rings of Saturn
flash by. We used to play for
nickels and dimes, now we play to
the sky, now we play to get high.
Music makes us fly...

FADE TO BLACK

END ACT I

ACT II

Scene 1:

As the lights come up, the sound of rain can be heard falling on the ashes in the valley. Rain falling on the flames in the city. Rain falling on the mad mob racing wildly through the streets. The rain falls as tears of sadness, down upon the pain of the souls of Styx Alley. The mad mob screams in memory of yesterday as the avenues dissolve in avalanches of mud. A moving caravan of bodies and bottles, pouring down into the valley, covering everything. Only wet ashes remain of the tenements. Only wet ashes remain, as the mountain of mud rolls into the valley, drowning all the drunken raiders. The sound of breaking bottles falls all around, bits of broken glass cover the rocky ground.

We see a rooftop scene. MERK and THE SHADES, with ANGEL, RUBY, REAPER and EBONY are hiding out on the rooftop of the Styx Bar, which rises above the alley. They are watching the deluge of mud in the valley. RUBY and EBONY settle down on the top of the roof with old man REAPER. The three of them figure out what they'll need at the store. RUBY counts off the things on her fingers, as REAPER says them to her and EBONY repeats the words...

> ANGEL
> (singing softly "Lost in a Tragedy")
> Grew up in the projects, hard and
> lean, fighting in the streets,
> making the scene... Just another
> casualty, lost in a tragedy

ANGEL (cont.)
Spent time on the needle, living
the silent scream, got lost in the
neon gleam, learned how to hustle,
learned how to scheme, learned how
to be heard, but not seen...
　　Real gone kid, party dream,
just another casualty, lost in a
tragedy
　　Suddenly got clean, went to
work in a factory, saved the pay,
moved away...
　　Real gone kid, party dream,
just another casualty, lost in a
tragedy...

ANGEL stops singing and looks up at the sky
reflectively. We hear the mantra of the weird
family, RUBY, REAPER, and EBONY.

REAPER
Coffins.

RUBY
Coffins.

EBONY
Coffins.

REAPER
Shovels.

RUBY
Shovels.

EBONY
Shovels.

REAPER
Funeral pyres.

RUBY
Funeral pyres.

                    EBONY
Funeral pyres.

                         REAPER
   Grenades.

                        RUBY
   Grenades.

                         EBONY
   Grenades.

                        REAPER
   Prisons.

                        RUBY
   Prisons.

                        EBONY
   Prisons.

                         REAPER
   Missiles.

                        RUBY
   Missiles.

                        EBONY
   Missiles.

                         REAPER
   Bombs.

                        RUBY
   Bombs.

                        EBONY
   Bombs.

                         REAPER
Germ warfare.

                        RUBY
Germ warfare.

EBONY
(stumbling over the long word)
Germ War Fare...Germ War Fare,
Germ War Fare...

As the ghastly chant dies down, ANGEL starts telling of the hype he'd once known a long time ago, and of how he'd lived then.

A synthesizer keyboard with swing beat can be played offstage to arrest the dreamlike quality of "The Purple Hood Piano Suite"; also a bongo beat on synthesizer keyboard with "Purple Hood Suite" notes, if desired, would liven up the piece.

ANGEL
(speaking "Angel's Lament")
I remember hotels, jazz joints,
jobs, work, taxes, books, songs,
instruments...
    There's this hype I used to
know, a long time ago. He's still
out there, looking for magic in a
$10 bag and somebody else's piece
of plastic. Yeah, he's still out
there looking for magic, in the
Haight Ashbury's pitiful and
tragic third eye...
    He's still out there, looking
for magic in the place children
call hell...he's a street corner
junkie, with no one but a kid to
call honey...yeah, just another
street corner junkie, with an
electric violin, trying to find
out where the nightmare ends and
the daydream begins...yeah...

MERK and THE SHADES saunter over to ANGEL's corner to contribute to the monologue, turning it into a dialogue...

                    MERK
          There's bodies turning up in
          Philly, some strangled, some
          O.D.'d, bodies of wasted druggies
          being dragged out for all to
          see...

One of THE SHADES steps forward as he speaks,
followed by the others.

                    SHADE 1
          Hidden in a shooting gallery, done
          in by the dealer man, too many
          junkies 'round, like too many
          flies in a pan...yeah, too many
          junkies 'round, like too many
          flies in a pan...

                    SHADE 2
          Gotta keep the cash flow going,
          gotta keep 'em working, cash flow
          part of the plan...

                    SHADE 3
          Ain't no pension plan, strike
          option, or retirement pay for
          junkies who owe the man, ain't
          nothing but death for druggies
          that into the man...

                    SHADE 4
          Seven bodies found so far in a
          shooting gallery in Philly. Some
          strangled, some O.D.'d, some just
          died of disease...

                    THE SHADES
                    (chorus)
          Seven bodies found, wasted,
          strangled, O.D.'d...in a tenement
          slum in Philly.

> THE SHADES (cont.)
> Poor old junkies don't get no
> cemetery, just like the Jews of
> World War II, old junkies get
> dumped in a ditch...some say
> that's okay.

THE SHADES saunter over to RUBY's place on the
roof. They could dance over as the sad, slow
music plays in the background. SHADE 1
continues the story, closer to the girl, that
she might be sure to hear what they're talking
about.

> SHADE 1
> Dealer man, may be a pimp, some
> say...

> SHADE 2
> Some say he knows what turned
> those poor bodies back into clay.

> SHADE 3
> He knows what happened to those
> ladies that day...

> SHADE 4
> That day when they couldn't pay...

> RUBY
> (looking at THE SHADES, then over to ANGEL)
> What were you saying about that
> guy who played the electric
> violin, a long time ago?

> ANGEL
> He's still looking for a pot of
> gold at the end of the rainbow.
> He's still out there looking for
> magic in a $10 bag. He's still
> out there, trying to get high.

> ANGEL (cont.)
> (looks directly at RUBY)
> All he does is shoot and tie!
> Someday he's gonna get a hot shot
> and die. Yeah, someday, he's
> gonna get a hot shot and die...

RUBY puts her hands over EBONY's ears and draws him closer, while REAPER inspects the tattoos that he has on his hands, arms, and legs. Then he gets up and goes over to the other side of the rooftop, where ANGEL's gun is, now nicely polished and reassembled. REAPER picks it up and holds it over the rooftop, aiming it at the sky. Looking for a high-flying bird to hit on the fly. MERK stands up from his slouched position on the roof and walks around, talking, while gesturing with his head.

> MERK
> Up there in the burnt-out town,
> down there in the valley, there
> were shooting galleries, where
> everyone was using outfits and
> matches, with little silver cooker
> spoons. Using valium to hold off
> cold turkey, looking for smack,
> settling for anything able to be
> found, anything able to be scored
> on the street...knowing it's hell
> and nobody cares, 'cause the stuff
> makes you feel that you haven't a
> care. Yeah, stuff makes you feel
> like everything's okay everywhere.

MERK goes over to RUBY, kneels down next to her, almost whispering in her ear but loud enough for the roof to hear, while taking one of her arms.

                    MERK
      When you don't have it, you shake
      and tear your hair...sometimes
      your skin feels bad, 'cause coming
      down's something bad...you feel
      there's bugs crawling on you
      everywhere. You get the shakes,
      hallucinate. You're wasted and
      almost senile. You go crazy and
      get infections that make you
      scream with pain. You're just
      another broken child lost in the
      world again, with nothing left but
      ruin and shame. Locked into a
      life shattered by disease,
      poverty, despair. Knowing there
      ain't no relief, and nothing but
      another shot to look forward to...
          Nothing but another empty
      day, another dead night, when
      there's nothing left to do but
      fix, 'cause all a junkie has to do
      is get high, all a junkie has to
      do is just score, just once
      more...there ain't no final
      score...

Synthesizer on swing can have drumbeats
increase, in back of "Purple Hood Suite" music
on synthesizer.

RUBY shakes off MERK's hand, gets up and with
the child, EBONY, moves away to the other side
of the roof where REAPER is, but MERK's voice
follows her as he gets up and moves to the
middle of the roof, where he addresses the gang.

                    MERK
      Some people start out playing and
      singing, dancing and writing, but
      it don't last. The needle's a
      jealous lover. Horse don't want
      no other. It's got an insatiable
      urge to stay high.

MERK (cont.)
Horse don't never say goodbye. It
just sighs, say, don't you wanna
get high?
Yeah, horse don't never say
goodbye.

The synthesizer beat accentuates the words
dumdedadopaduduas, as THE SHADES, ANGEL and
REAPER snap their fingers and do a ballet
breakdance about a junkie trying to score, and
then doing up in pantomime, like a shooting
gallery full of mimes. RUBY returns to her
abject position of cuddling EBONY and scratching
her arms and legs, shivering with chills.

ANGEL
(to RUBY)
You asked me about that hype!
He's looking for magic in a
$10 bag. Looking for magic to
keep him alive. Looking for a
lost piece of plastic to take care
of his habit for a few nights.
The kid's getting older, he don't
go to school, his daddy makes the
rules. He runs free through the
streets of the city, sometimes
sells crack to other kids, the
ones that go to school. Brings
the money home and gives it to his
daddy, who uses it for smack!
Ain't that pretty? That's what
you gonna do with Ebony? Or maybe
you gonna sell him for a hit
someday, when your body's too old
to pay!
He's still out there, with no
place to go. He's still out
there, another lost soul, killing
time, strung out on a dime, with
bruises and scabs on his arms and
needle marks on his mind.

ANGEL (cont.)
He's still out there, losing time.
Struggling to survive, so he can
do up just one more time, just one
more time. That's all he lives
for, that next score. Cop, fix,
it's only a dime, then there's
nothing to do but wait for the
next time...
      Yeah, 'cause that's what a
street hype does, can't afford
nothing else, with just a tiny
check for him and the kid. Like a
broken violin, playing a tune so
forlorn, with only the thought for
another good time. That's the
only thing on a strung-out hype's
mind, only thing on a strung-out
hype's mind, is how to get the
next shot for another good time...
      Yeah, that's the only thing
on a strung-out hype's mind, how
to get that next dime for another
good time.

As the lights fade, the tableau of ANGEL, MERK,
THE SHADES, RUBY, EBONY, and REAPER dance the
dance of death on the roof, with REAPER holding
high the gun and the others with their arms
raised in the clenched fist salute of junkie
power. RUBY begins to sing "In This Lifetime"
as Act II fades.

                    RUBY
Night time, neon light time, makes
me wanta get so high, in the night
time...
      Shadow show time, how the
week does fly, weekend night,
stoned time, it's time to get
high...

> RUBY (cont.)
> In the night time, street life
> time, everybody's got a line,
> everybody's looking for a dime, in
> their own way.
>   Night time, neon light time,
> makes me wanta get so high, in
> this lifetime...

REAPER hands the gun to ANGEL, goes over to RUBY and speaks to her as the lights continue to fade.

> REAPER
> (putting his hand on RUBY's shoulder)
>   Honey, we're a long ways away from
> yesterday and those neon lights of
> Broadway, where carnival hucksters
> hawk their wares, along midways of
> cheap thrills and dares...
>   We're a long ways away from
> yesterday, a long ways away from
> Washington Square and Grant
> Avenue's Chinatown fair.
>   We're a long ways away from
> yesterday and the neon lights of
> Broadway... A long ways away from
> the trips of yesterday...a long
> ways away...

> RUBY
> C'mon, Man, I'm sick.

RUBY doubles over in a cough that shakes her whole body, as EBONY runs over crying.

> EBONY
> Mommy! Mommy!

FADE TO BLACK

END ACT II

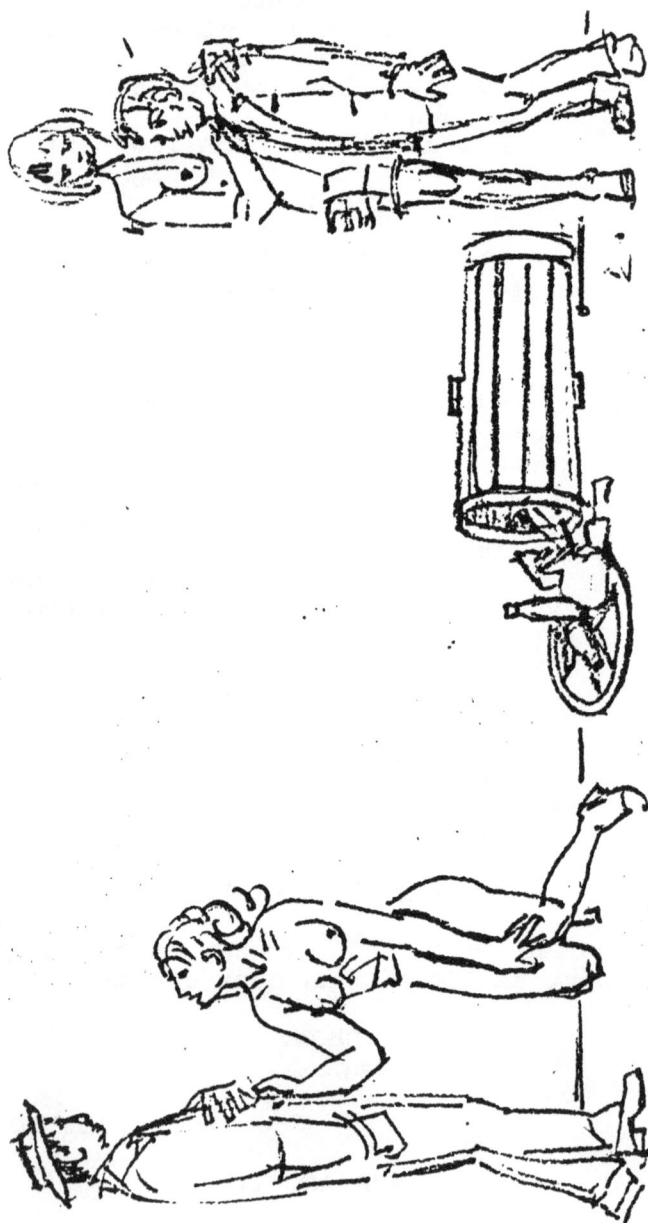

ACT III

Scene 1:

A sidewalk is lined with tenements, a liquor
store, a grocery/drug store, a pinball arcade, a
porno movie theater, a bar and pool hall. The
world of a Skid Row slum.   It could be 42nd
Street in New York City or The Tenderloin
District in San Francisco. The music coming
from the bar is honky-tonk piano blues that
sounds like neon.   It's midnight. Shadowy
figures drift back and forth along the sidewalk.

Tall, short...the darkness camouflages the
people of the night. A few figures, as three-
dimensional silhouettes, lean against the
outside of the storefronts waiting for
something. As one jukebox tune fades into
another, the strains of minor chords float into
the street and a bop-stepping shadow moves along
the sidewalk, dance-trotting to the beat of the
sweet street suite.

A modern Fagin is MERK, as he now appears as a
zoot-suited pied piper, master of illusion. The
dealer, MERK, comes with his legion of children,
THE SHADES, dressed up like punk rockers with
spiked hair, vests, jeans, chains, collars.
These kids are imitations of their leader, the
dealer, going down the street, bopping to the
beat, nodding to the figures hanging out against
the walls. The dealer turns around and, with a
wave of his hand, scatters THE SHADES following
him.   They disband, sauntering, slithering,
sliding up to the various customers waiting in
the shadows, hanging out in the doorsteps of the
sidewalk.

Out of the ghetto-blaster radio box MERK carries
comes a real cool and low rap.

>   GHETTO-BLASTER (O.S.)
> Whatcha want, we got it! Make
> your fantasy come true. C'mon
> now, whisper in my ear, have no
> fear. We'll make your dreams
> reality, take your pain away, make
> you free from care, have no
> fear...the dealer's here...the
> dealer's here!

>   THE SHADES
> C'mon now, whisper in my ear, have
> no fear, whatcha want, we got it,
> call it into the open air, this is
> the black market, anything you
> want, anytime, yeah, anything you
> want, anywhere, we got...we got...

Chorus dies down and MERK, the dealer, comes out
of the shadows.

>   MERK
>   (singing to THE SHADES)
> Whatcha want, name your fantasy,
> we'll take you there. Don't worry
> 'bout the fare. State your
> preference, we'll satisfy your
> every wish. Yeah, we'll make your
> dreams come true, take your pain
> away. Don't worry 'bout the
> price, don't worry 'bout the price
> today. We'll take it out in
> trade, so come on now. Tell us,
> whatcha want, we got it. Make
> your fantasy come true, whatcha
> want, we got it, call it out, or
> whisper it into my ear. C'mon
> now, whisper it in my ear, have no
> fear.

As MERK fades back into the shadows, THE SHADES
dance in and out of the lingering customers,

positioning themselves individually next to each
one, while chanting inquiringly.

                    THE SHADES
                (each to his customer)
          Hooka tooka, soda cracker, does
          your momma chaw tobacca? If your
          momma chaw tobacca...Hooka tooka
          soda cracker...

MERK positions himself on one side of the stage.

                    MERK
                (in aside to audience)
          There's a crackdown going on in
          Crack Town, burning spoonfuls of
          baking soda...
               Somebody's cooking, cooking
          up a storm, burning spoonfuls of
          baking soda, sickly dry, sweet
          aroma, burning spoonfuls of baking
          soda...
               Somebody's cooking in Crack
          Town, heat wave sizzling all
          around, burning spoonfuls of
          baking soda.

                    SHADE 1
          Free-basing...

                    SHADE 2
          Tying...

                    SHADE 3
          Hitting...

                    SHADE 4
          Dying...

                    MERK
From snow white spoonfuls of
baking soda, burning spoonfuls of
baking soda, in Crack Town,
there's a crackdown going on,
burning spoonfuls of baking
soda...

MERK fades back into the shadows, as chorus of
THE SHADES can be heard again, chanting their
mantra of doom.

                  THE SHADES
Hooka tooka, soda cracker, does
your momma chaw tobacca?
        If your momma chaw tobacca,
hooka tooka, soda cracker...
        Step on a crack, break your
mother's back...
        Hooka tooka, soda cracker,
c'mon and get your crack...

As the shadowy silhouettes reach out their hands
to the chorus of THE SHADES who, in turn, hand
back to them small tinfoil packets of white
powder in exchange for dollars, one of the
SHADOWs steps into the light and addresses the
audience in an aside, as MERK did before, in a
song of explanation.

                   SHADOW
                 (of ANGEL)
We were living on the street,
working in the day...
        Playing on the rooftops every
night...twenty-four hours a day,
twenty-four hours a day, twenty-
four hours a day...
        People in the park, dealing
after dark, twenty-four hours a
day...But the music goes on
anyway...many kids died yesterday,
many kids die living this way...

SHADOW (cont.)
The road gets longer every
day...when you're living on the
streets, working in the day,
playing on the rooftops, twenty-
four hours in a day...the music
goes on anyway...many kids died
yesterday, many kids died living
on the streets, this way...
     Working in the day, playing
in the night, twenty-four hours in
a day...people in the park,
dealing after dark, the music goes
on anyway, the music goes on
anyway...

FADE TO BLACK

Scene 2:

The next day, in a tenement apartment with a
beat-up, battered couch, a wooden table and
chair. We see shadowy figures moving around in
the twilight of the moon coming through the
window-pane. The silhouettes, as dancers,
stretch, slump, bop, and then there comes a
knock on the door.

The door opens and in comes MERK, dressed in the
same manner as he was before, only in different
clothes, with a cane and no ghetto-blaster. He
has a plantation straw hat and a jacket. The
shadowy figures crowd around him as he moves
toward the table. He sits down in the chair and
removes white plastic containers of small
envelopes from his pockets.

The junkies form a line, putting their money on
the table and getting a white packet in
exchange. The ones who've already scored go off
into corners, separately or in groups of two or
three. They pull spoons from their pockets,
and matches. They put a little of the white

powder into the spoon, adding a drop or two of distilled water from an eyedropper. Then, a lit match goes under the spoon until the liquid gently dissolves the crystals. The needle is stuck into the spoon and sucks up the liquid into the body of the syringe. The junkie tightens the tourniquet he's placed around his upper arm to pump up a vein. When one pops up, swollen, he sticks the needle into the vein. Then he releases the liquid ever so slowly. The body slumps in temporary ecstasy.

                    REAPER
          (singing "In This Lifetime")
          Night time, neon light time, makes
          me wanna get so high, in the night
          time...
                Shadow show time, how the
          week does fly, weekend night,
          stoned time, it's time to get
          high...
                In the night time, street
          life time, everybody's got a line,
          everybody's looking for a dime, in
          their own way...
                Night time, neon light time,
          makes me wanna get so high, in
          this life time...

                     MERK
     (moving around to each junkie, asking)
          Can you hear the beat? When you
          feel the heat, move your feet!
          Yeah, you've gotta learn to move
          your feet, in time to the beat...
                Can you hear the beat, as it
          rolls along the street, as it
          flies through the sky, up above
          our eyes...

                    SHADE 1
          Oh, so high...

                    SHADE 2
          Yeah!

MERK goes around to all the junkies, asking each
one how they feel and listening to their
answers, to make sure they haven't O.D.'d. The
then goes over to RUBY, who's slumped on the
floor, resting, in the corner of the room.

                    MERK
           (touching RUBY's head)
        Can you hear the beat? When you
        feel the heat, move your feet, in
        time to the beat... Can you hear
        the beat, as it rolls along the
        street, as it flies through the
        sky, up above our eyes?

                    RUBY
        (raising her eyes, answering)
        Oh, so high, so very, very high...

                    MERK
        Yeah!

MERK goes over to SHADE 3 (another junkie), who
is plucking an old acoustic six-string guitar,
making a melody to accompany MERK's words.

                    MERK
           (singing "City Lights")
        Have you seen the City Lights?
        Have you been to town? Have you
        danced up and down Haight Street
        in a velvet gown? Have you
        laughed and played and sung? Are
        you still having fun?

                    SHADE 3
           (singing "City Lights")
        Have you seen the City Lights now?
        Have you been to town? Have you
        danced up and down Haight Street
        in a velvet gown?
           Can you hear the beat? When
        you feel the heat, move your feet,
        yeah...you've gotta learn to move
        your feet in time to the beat...

SHADE 3 (cont.)
Can you hear the beat, as it rolls
along the street, as it flies
through the sky, up above our
eyes, oh, so high, yeah...
     By a happy child, have fun,
stay young, play in the sun. Life
is sad, life is mad, life is love,
life is breath, after life there's
only death...
     Have you laughed and played
and sung, are you still having
fun...staying high, oh, so high...

MERK
(touching SHADE 3's head)
Be a happy child, have fun, stay
young, play in the sun! Life is
sad, life is mad, life is love,
life is breath...
(grasps SHADE 3's shoulders, looks into eyes)
     After life, there's only
death...

MERK continues down the line of bodies slumped
against the walls, making sure none have O.D.'d
while SHADE 3 plays again on the accoustic
guitar, which we hear in the background.

SHADE 3
Have you seen the City Lights now?
Have you been to town? Have you
danced up and down Haight Street
in a velvet gown?
     Can you hear the beat? When
you feel the heat, move your feet,
yeah...You've gotta learn to move
your feet in time to the beat.
     Can you hear the beat, as it
rolls along the street, as it
flies through the sky, up above
our eyes, oh, so high, yeah...

FADE TO BLACK

Scene 3:

Dim pastel lights come up on a cell block in a jailhouse. As the lights brighten a little, the figure in the cell in the middle of the stage approaches the bars. It is MERK, only now he is dressed in jailhouse clothes. He puts his hands on the bars and sings "The Jail House Blues" song. A parade of guards and prisoners pass before the cell. Prisoners are dressed in blue-and-white striped uniforms; guards are in blue police uniforms.

>   MERK
> Jail House Blues, Jail House
> Blues, from the top of my head to
> the soles of my shoes, living with
> the Jail House Blues... Been
> inside for six years now, been
> inside so long, just decided to
> make up a song...
>   Looking out through steel
> bars, gray skies are all I see,
> with the Jail House Blues for
> company...
>   Jail House Blues all around
> me...
>   Ain't never any end to paying
> dues, when you're living with the
> Jail House Blues...

MERK finishes his song and slinks back to the cot in his cell. The light passes on to the next cell, where SHADE 3 is seen, dancing in circles in his cell, singing "We Flew" to himself.

>   SHADE 3
> We flew into the sun, we
> transcended time, becoming ghostly
> people; some thought death our
> only design...

SHADE 3 (cont.)
As fantasies and oriental myths,
changed the outlines of our
lives...
We were looking for a space,
we found a place, while becoming
we lived a pan...to...mime...
Wandering through the shadows,
dancing to rhymes, mystic
silhouettes lost in visions of
another clime...

While the light fades in SHADE 3's cell, it
brightens on the figure of an approaching GUARD,
who swings his flashlight as he walks, a la
Charlie Chaplin. He stops and shines his light
into MERK's cell, then into SHADE 3's, mumbles
to himself, then begins singing "Lost in a
Tragedy." He checks the cells to make sure
there are bodies inside.

GUARD
(shaking his head
Never had a chance...just another
casualty, lost in a tragedy...

GUARD continues his rounds, shining his
flashlight on the sleeping bodies behind the
steel bars as SHADE 3 plucks a guitar in the
darkness.

GUARD
Grew up in the projects, hard and
lean, fighting in the streets,
making the scene...
Just another casualty, lost
in a tragedy... Spent time on the
needle, living the silent scream.
Got lost in the neon gleam,
learned how to hustle, learned how
to scheme, learned how to be
heard, but not seen...

>   GUARD (cont.)
>   Real gone kid, party dream...
>   Just another casualty, lost in a
>   tragedy...
>   Suddenly got clean, went to
>   work in a factory, saved the pay,
>   moved away.
>   Real gone kid, party dream,
>   just another casualty, lost in a
>   tragedy...

As GUARD turns a corner of the tier that takes him offstage, we hear the sound of the guitar and REAPER's voice coming from the darkness also.

>   REAPER
>   Walking down the street, feeling
>   so forlorn, remembering twenty
>   years ago, another March
>   morn...another March morn...
>   We'd been drinking burgundy
>   for many a day, yeah, we'd been
>   sharing a bottle to keep the blues
>   away... Yeah, then you went to
>   the hospital and I was left all
>   alone, with nothing but a needle
>   and a dealer to call home...
>   Nothing but a needle and a
>   dealer to call home...
>   Looking at the sky now, and
>   the glass upon the ground,
>   watching the wind dance the ashes
>   all around, yeah, there's glass on
>   the ground, glass all over the
>   ground...

As REAPER's song fades off, we see the beam of the flashlight as the GUARD returns on his second round, singing another song as the piano music of memory plays in the background. He's singing softly, as though rocking a baby to sleep with a sweet lullaby.

                GUARD
You better be careful what you do,
or they're gonna have a card on
you...
       Yeah, or they're gonna have a
card on you...
       So you better not steal and
you better not shout, don't get so
drunk that you can't hang
out...don't get mad and punch
anyone out...
       Don't get caught with joints
or stuff, don't sell dope to a
narc, beware of people you don't
know. I'm sure you've heard all
this before, but hear it again...
       Stay free and clear of the
jail house door...
       You better be careful what
you do, or they're gonna have a
card on you, yeah...
       Better be careful what you
do, or they're gonna have a card
on you...

The GUARD finishes his rounds and once again
reaches the end of his watch and disappears
offstage. The piano music fades. As the lights
of the cell block dim, we hear a haunting
version on piano of "Twenty-four Hours In a
Day," improvised saxophone and notes played on
electric bass guitar...sung by RUBY...who we
last saw in the shooting gallery...she never
made it to the penitentiary... She O.D.'d.

                RUBY
We were living on the streets,
working in the days, playing on
the rooftops every night...
       Twenty-four hours in a day,
there's only twenty-four hours in
a day...

                    RUBY (cont.)
People in the park, dealing after
dark, twenty-four hours a
day...twenty-four hours in a day,
the music goes on anyway, the
music goes on anyway...
         Many kids die living this
way, many kids died yesterday,
many kids die living on the
streets today...
         The music goes on anyway, the
music goes on anyway...
         We're working in the day,
playing in the night, there's only
twenty-four hours in a day, only
twenty-four hours in a day...

As the voice and sound drift off into eternity,
the set is a deep purple maze of labyrinthian
cages...and then deeper purple until even the
shadows...

                              FADE TO BLACK

        END ACT III

            FINIS

ROOFTOPS

THE STORY OF STREET MUSICIANS IN SAN FRANCISCO, CALIFORNIA IN THE 1970s and 1980s

Set in and around the environs of an inner-city people's park, we watch a small group of friends gently swimming in the currents of life on the outskirts of the mainstream. As they comment on the larger world, they also lay their plans to move from where they find themselves to a higher plane. While Ruby and Reaper are long gone, the world they inhabited is still around; these people know of it, but are not yet its victims, and may not be if the hope and kindness of those living in the park bear lasting fruit...

celebrating insanity, 'cause the world was obviously crazy,
totally out of its mind...kids running wild in the
streets, killing each other, playing chicken for treats,
halloween was all the time in 1959...

beatniks reflecting on beatitudes
on the cover of Time and Life magazines, in the style of
bohemia, existing in a pantomime...poetry was on the street
and in the bar, on the sidewalk, in the car...

remember literature, remember rhyme, remember jazz, when
you cry out the story of the times, remember kid, 'cuz
you'se a whiz, just lie those joints and jays away...
lie about the needles and the scores for dope, lie
about the time you spent highing without hope...

CAST:

CLIO   Ageless woman, in reality the Muse of History incognito as a musician

BONES   A 37 year old woman, former junkie, now alcoholic

LEGS   A 35 year old skinny woman, junkie derelict punk

JAY   A 35 year old hippie drug dealer

PUNK   A punk musician

ROCKER   A rock 'n' roll musician

FOLKIE   A folk singer

THE GRIM REAPER   A black-cloaked figure

POLICEMAN

SETTING:
The latter part of the twentieth century, San Francisco. A western town in the northern part of the state of California, U.S.A.

SETS:

Act 1, Scene 1   A rooftop
Act 1, Scene 2   A city street
Act 2, Scene 1   People's Park
Act 3, Scene 1   Market Street
Act 4, Scene 1   Entrance of the Warfield Theater, Market Street

ACT I

Scene 1:

A rooftop scene in early evening. The colors of twilight blue play counterpoint to the melody of "Rooftops" sounding from a piano offstage. PUNK, visible only as a shadowy figure, plays the guitar on the roof. Another shadow emerges. This is all seen through a scrim or filmy curtain.

The piano music fades away. The scrim rises. PUNK is a young musician playing a riff on an electric guitar. A WOMAN emerges from the door leading into the tenemant. She stealthily creeps onto the front of the roof to exit via a fire escape ladder that leads offstage. As she goes down the ladder, a POLICEMAN enters the roof with a drawn revolver, looking for her.

The guitar melody tapers off slowly and is picked up and duplicated by the piano and piano harp offstage.

                    FADE TO BLACK AS:

The music from "Broadway Blues" comes from offstage.

Scene 2:

A city street, clearly a Skid Row district.

This street is awake twenty-four hours a day. On the street: The Warfield Theatre, a rock 'n' roll emporium where acts perform nightly; two hotels; a mission that feeds people, with a line of waifs, bums, vagabonds and runaways in the evenings; across the street from the hotels is a park, known as People's Park... It is open all the time, with green benches and wooden picnic tables, a small stage, and barbed wire behind it.

PUNK and LEGS are sitting on the street.

CLIO, ghost of time, Muse of History, appears on the set. She carries a tambourine which she plays as though she were a dervish from Hades. Then, in a more subdued fashion, she drops the instrument and dances and sings a song explaining the dereliction and apathy of the characters in this play...while wandering back and forth along the city street, always checking her tambourine to see if anyone has put money in it.

CLIO
(singing "Hiroshima, Nagasaki, 1945")

> Hiroshima, Nagasaki, 1945. God sighed, the world cried, children preferred suicide!
> We have so many weapons with which to kill and help us die. Why do we so want to die? Is death the ultimate high?
> San Francisco, California, 1965. Golden Outfit was the king. Lady Crystal was the queen. They ruled the kingdom of the streets.
> Over the children they reigned supreme... Death was the ultimate high. Junkies, jesters, with hypodermic sceptres wandered the plastic cities as synthetically angelic guides, pursuing suicide.
> We have so many weapons with which to kill and help us die. Why do we so want to die?

CLIO (cont.)
Is death the ultimate high?
Only love will help us to survive.
Let's give love a try...

As the song ends, CLIO picks up the tambourine, puts the change in it into her bodice and floats offstage through the park.

FADE TO BLACK:

END ACT I

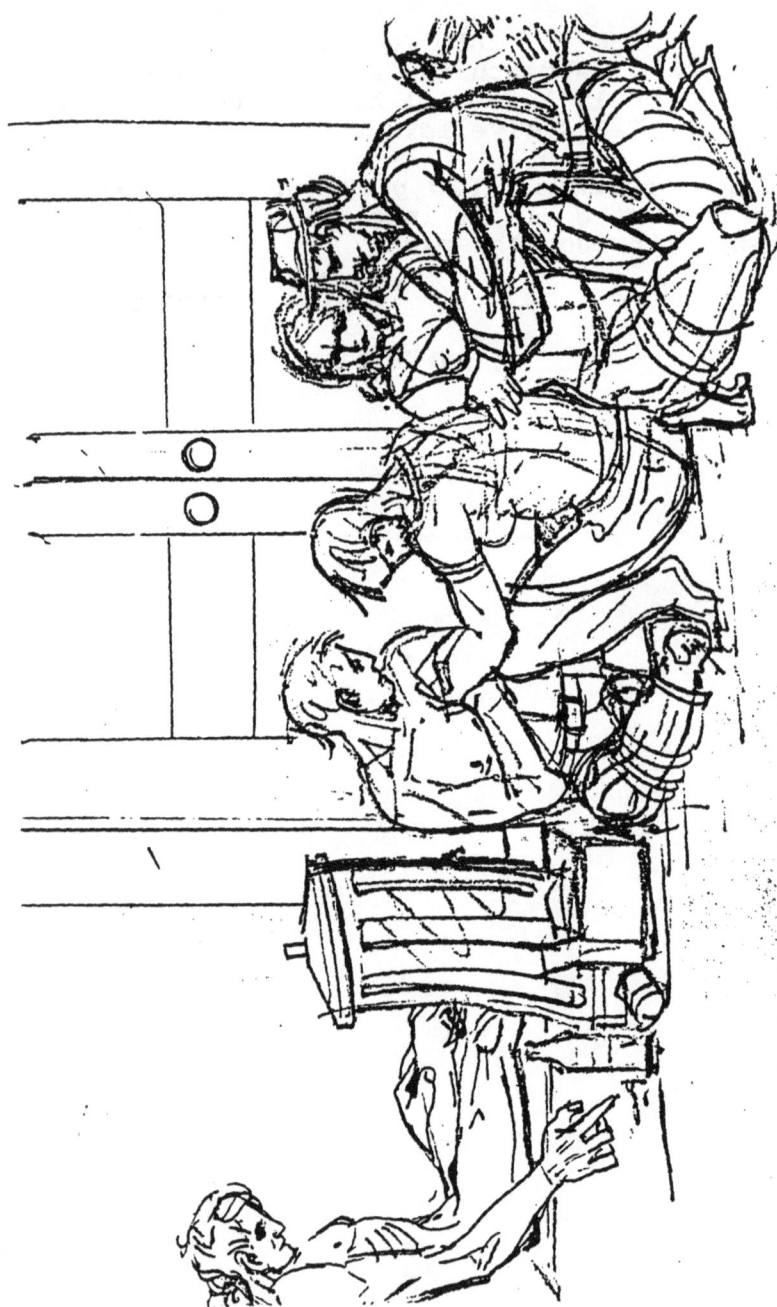

ACT II

Scene 1:

People's Park at the coming of evening.

A misty haze envelops the park. There are green benches and picnic tables. In one corner stands a small stage, behind it a barbed wire fence encircling the park. Upstage is a candy store with a door opening into backstage.

PUNK struts into the park carrying his guitar on his back. LEGS and BONES are sitting on one of the benches talking in low tones, while JAY wanders around from table to table, occasionally calling out, "Joints!" He is looking for someone to buy a jay. FOLKIE and ROCKER are sitting on a bench across from LEGS and BONES, tuning their guitars and warming up with a blue jazz, folk rock country sound. PUNK gets up on the stage.

> PUNK
> (singing "Last Year")
> Left town 'bout a year ago. They
> was busting all the junkies, now
> don'tcha know...
> We used to score in the park,
> and on the street. Suddenly our
> connections were heat. We
> couldn't get no dope. We couldn't
> be like we used to be...
> We'd score in the park, we'd
> score on the street. Suddenly,
> everyone was the heat.

PUNK (cont.)
We'd go to Skid Row, we'd look at
the beats, we'd look at the heat,
they're all around, everywhere,
don'tcha know...
    Look at the heat, look at the
heat. Heat was everywhere,
everywhere, everywhere,
everywhere. We couldn't get
nothing too sweet...
    Everybody knows the heat was
all over the streets, all over
those streets, busting everybody
that looked beat, busting
everybody that looked scared,
yeah.
    They were busting everybody
that year, busting in the park,
busting on the sidewalk, busting
everybody. The heat was all over
the street. It was hot out there,
yeah, it was hot.
    It was the year of the heat,
the year of the heat, busting all
the beats...

PUNK ends his song and goes to sit with FOLKIE
and ROCKER, all three gently playing their
guitars as BONES gets up from her seat on the
bench and goes up on the little stage.

BONES
(talking/singing "There's Babies Crying")
    There's babies crying, people
dying, hunger's everywhere.
    Say, there's babies crying,
people dying, hunger's everywhere.
    The world needs help, needs
money, food, love and
understanding. The world needs
the necessities of life.

                    BONES (cont.)
                      (to LEGS)
Take back your life, honey, take
back your life. Take back your
life...

                    ROCKER
         (singing "We Plow Food")
We plow food back into the fields.
We throw food away. We could give
it away. We could give it away.
We could teach people how to grow.
We could teach people how to live
instead of how to kill. Instead
of teaching war, we could teach
love instead. We could teach
love, instead teach love, instead.
Why don't we teach some love
instead?
         There's babies dying, people
crying, all over Earth.
Starvation, poverty, disease and
despair, brutality, war... Why
don't we love each other any more?

LEGS stands and dances around the park.

                    LEGS
    (talking/singing "Rich Get Richer")
         Rich get richer, poor get poorer.
There's hunger everywhere.
There's hunger everywhere. Greedy
get greedier, the gold gets
colder. We don't give nothing
away no more. We got plenty, we
got plenty that we don't need. We
got enough to share...

JAY walks over to where LEGS ends up and walks
her back to her bench.

>   JAY
>   (singing "The People Song")
>   People. There's people selling
>   people. Everywhere there's people
>   buying and selling people.
>   There's slavery everywhere. We're
>   shocked by our indifference, our
>   brutality. Sometimes seems we
>   care more about things than people
>   today...

JAY stops to roll a cigarette.

>   JAY, BONES, LEGS, ROCKER, FOLKIE & PUNK
>   (singing "The People Song")
>   People, people, people... Ain't
>   nothing wrong with being people,
>   people, people... There's people
>   everywhere. Short and tall, fat
>   and thin, black and white, yellow,
>   red, brown, rich and poor...
>   There's people everywhere. Old
>   and young. There's all kinds of
>   different people everywhere...
>   We gotta live together. We
>   gotta help each other. We gotta
>   share our stuff. We gotta learn
>   to care about each other if we're
>   gonna share... There's people
>   everywhere...

BONES and LEGS panhandle. JAY sits at the table
rolling cigarettes. PUNK, ROCKER and FOLKIE
play guitar. BONES, LEGS and JAY alternately,
concurrently and singly sing, as a medieval
madrigal sing-song round, each adding their
voice at the right moment.

LEGS
(singing "Spare Change")
Spare change, spare change, spare
change. You got any spare change,
share change. We need a billion,
you got a million, you got a few
thousand, you got a grand...?
    Spare change, share change,
spare change, share change...

BONES
(singing "Wall Street")
Oh, when the lights went out on
Wall Street, all the elevators got
stuck, the pages were frustrated,
not knowing which end was up...
    Oh, when the lights went out
on Wall Street, the money power
play came to an end that day...

JAY
(singing "Gold is Cold")
Gold is cold, gold is old, gold is
gold, gold has never cried, gold
has never lied, gold has never
died...

BONES
(still singing "Wall Street")
There was a blackout in the Stock
Exchange. They couldn't see the
names on the Board. We can't make
money that way... What we gonna
do to make some pay?
    Oh, when the lights went out
on Wall Street, there was a
blackout on the Stock Exchange.
Oh, what a day that was. No one
could read the ticker-tape, or
count the interest rate...

                    BONES (cont.)
      Oh, when the lights went out on
      Wall Street, no one could see the
      Exchange, all the percentages were
      thrown off balance, all the stocks
      were out of range...

                    LEGS
       (still singing "Spare Change")
       Spare change, share change, spare
       change. You got any spare change
       to share?
             Share change. We need
       millions, you got billions, we
       need thousands, you got millions.
       Share change, spare change, share
       change, spare change.

JAY, watching, gestures her over to buy some
cigarettes with that dollar. He dances up to
her, cigarette hanging from his own mouth.

                    JAY
       (still singing "Gold is Cold")
       Gold is cold, gold is old, gold is
       gold... Gold has never cried,
       gold has never lied, gold has
       never died...
             Did you make your gold today?
       Have you had your gold today?
       Gold is gold, gold is cold, gold
       is old... Gold has never lied,
       gold has never cried, gold never
       dies...

BONES tries to divert LEGS from buying
cigarettes because she wants a bottle of wine.
She reaches for the dollar LEGS is waving at
JAY...

BONES
(still singing "Wall Street")
Oh, when the lights went out on
Wall Street, all the elevators got
stuck, the pages were frustrated,
not knowing which end was up...
Oh, when the lights went out
on Wall Street, the money power
play came to an end that day.
There was a blackout on the
Stock Exchange. They couldn't see
the names on the Board. We can't
make money that way. What we
gonna do to make some pay...
Oh, when the lights went out
on Wall Street, there was a
blackout on the Stock Exchange.
Oh, what a day that was. No
one could read the ticker-tape, or
count the interest rate...
Oh, when the lights went out
on Wall Street, no one could see
the Exchange. All the percentages
were thrown off balance, all the
stocks were out of range...

BONES is unable to distract LEGS from buying the
cigarette with their only dollar. As the
cigarette passes from the hand of JAY to the
hand of LEGS and the dollar passes from the hand
of LEGS to the hand of JAY, BONES waits
patiently for LEGS to light the cigarette. LEGS
then takes a long drag from it, passes it to
BONES, who does the same, and passes it to
ROCKER and PUNK and FOLKIE, who all take drags
from it, finally passing it back to LEGS, who
takes the final drag and puts the filter out on
the bench.

We hear a piano playing blue jazz floating
through the air, as though from a piano bar up
the street from the park. ROCKER, PUNK and
FOLKIE all play their guitars.

111

                    JAY
         (singing "It's a Blue Country")
          It's a blue country, folks, when
          only the dealer man knows the
          score, 'cause he's the one with
          the candy store. In the
          underground it's the only grocery
          around...
               We don't need no stamps to
          get our plants. We grow
          everything ready-made, just like
          in the good old days...
               We've come a long ways from
          the good old days...
     (musical interlude of a bar played twice)
               There's people starving in
          the welfare lines; poverty is
          their only crime. They ain't done
          nothing wrong. They pay with
          their lives for the time spent
          waiting in line. It's not their
          fault, they just broke at the
          time...
               They might have been rich
          yesterday. Now, they standing
          around begging for dimes. Relief
          brings nothing but grief. Anybody
          knows that who's been there...
               Up, down, turn around, go
          into the underground, where only
          the dealer man knows the score.
          Only the dealer man knows the
          score. He's the one with the
          candy store, the only grocery on
          the block...

                              FADE TO BLACK

Scene 2:

People's Park the next morning. LEGS, BONES, ROCKER, PUNK, FOLKIE and JAY are all sitting together at a long table. JAY rolls his cigarettes, as usual. The three musicians strum lightly on their guitars.

>   LEGS
>   (to BONES)
> Why don't we form an act? Them
> playing, we could sing and dance
> our troubles away like we used to
> do in the old days. In the old
> days. We got a show, we do it all
> the time, don'tcha know. We're
> always out here playing and
> singing for cigarettes and wine.
> We could get our act together now,
> with the musicians, and we could
> go live on the rooftops and make a
> penthouse scene, instead of always
> hanging around People's Park. We
> could move to the rooftops. Do
> you know what I mean?

LEGS gets up and goes around to the upstage side of the table to act out her dream to her friends. To get them interested, she dances and sings her idea while they play and watch.

>   LEGS
>   (singing "Rooftops")
> Been thinking of moving to the
> rooftops today. Looking for a
> penthouse to take me away from the
> madness and distress of existence
> here...
>   Been looking, looking,
> looking everywhere. All I seem to
> see are shadows in the air,
> shadows in the air, shadows in the
> air...

                    LEGS (cont.)
All I seem to see are shadows in
the air, shadows everywhere...
        Looking, looking, looking
everywhere. Skeletons dancing all
around, there's skeletons all over
the town.
        Looks like a graveyard down
here, with skeletons dancing
everywhere...

BONES, catching her drift, decides to get into
the act and gets up to slide over to JAY...

                    BONES
    (singing part of "Needle")
How many dead and gone? How many
dead and gone? How many died with
a needle in their arm?
        How many died with a needle
in their arm? How many dead and
gone?

The musicians pick up the melody from BONES'
singing. LEGS sits down on the other side of
JAY, the two women trapping him between them,
rubbing his arms and his chest, wheedling a
cigarette from him. JAY gives LEGS a cigarette
for dancing and singing and entertaining him.

                    JAY
(singing part of "Needle" warningly to LEGS)
        Old junkies, they just waste away,
        living the concentration camp
        blues everyday. That's the price
        you gotta pay for the life you
        live with the needle anyway, gotta
        needle in your arm, wanna needle
        in your arm?

LEGS stares at him blankly. BONES, hearing the
way the conversation is going, decides to get in
on the act, warning her friend in her own way.

BONES
(singing part of "Needle" to LEGS)
Scoring, tripping, copping,
spiking, tying, fixing... You
wanna needle in your arm? You
wanna monkey on your back? You
wanna monkey on your back, honey,
baby, child? You wanna be some
mother's junkie brat?

JAY
(still singing)
You gotta hundred bucks a day,
now? You gotta hundred bucks a
day, say? You need a hundred
bucks a day to support your habit
anyway. You wanna golden arm to
kill you someday?

BONES
(still singing)
Barbed wire everywhere. It's a
concentration camp. It's a hippy
children's concentration camp
blues with barbed wire everywhere.
It's the cigarettes they fear.
They don't know the good magic of
the weed they fear... You just
smoke your cigarette, dear,
there's nothing in that sweet gold
to kill your mind...

JAY
(still singing)
Needle in your arm. You wanna
needle in your arm?

LEGS
Don't do no harm to put a needle
in your arm...

                    BONES
                (still singing)
          Now don't you put no needle in
          your arm...

                     JAY
                (still singing)
          Don't you put no needle in your
          arm...

ROCKER, PUNK, FOLKIE, JAY and BONES surround
LEGS, who sinks slowly to the ground, stunned by
their words and music.

          JAY, BONES, PUNK, FOLKIE & ROCKER
             (singing part of "Needle")
          You wanna save your arm, you wanna
          save your arm, save your arm now,
          child. Don't you put no needle in
          your arm...

                    BONES
          (motions the boys away from LEGS)
          Look at Lady Day. She passed away
          waiting for a needle in her arm,
          on a New York City Hospital bed
          one day. There was police all
          around her bed all day, waiting
          for her to try and stick a needle
          in her arm...
               Poor Lady Day, she passed
          away. She'd stuck too many
          needles in her arm...

                     JAY
          (rising and heading for the candy store)
          Candy store, candy store, candy
          store. Across the street there's
          a candy store...
                    (to LEGS)
               You like sugar, you like
          honey, you just like tea, you like
          Coke, what would you like it to
          be?

JAY ducks into the store, gets a bottle of wine and comes back, passing the bottle around the table.

> LEGS
> (singing "Voodoo Man")
> Saw the voodoo man. He's a magic
> man. Say, "child, got the
> medicine for you. Got the
> medicine for you, right here. Got
> the medicine for you, child, it
> will put away your blues. Child,
> got the medicine for you."

The musicians play streamlined acid blues. BONES joins in the song.

> LEGS & BONES
> (singing "Voodoo Man")
> He's a magic man, voodoo man. Got
> that medicine in his hand, got the
> medicine in his hand. He's a
> magic man, he's a voodoo man,
> coming with the medicine in his
> hand. He's a candy store man,
> he's a mother, he's a brother,
> he's a magic man, he's a voodoo
> man. Look! Ain't that him a'
> comin' with the medicine in his
> hand?

> JAY
> (drinks; sings "On the Street" to LEGS)
> Go out on the street, think you
> walk so sweet. Go out on the
> street, think you walk so sweet.
> You go out on the street, walk it
> sweet, on the street.

> BONES
> (sings same song to LEGS in agreement with JAY)
> You ain't got no money, ain't got
> no honey, ain't got no baby at
> all.

                    BONES (cont.)
You looking for a job, gotta pay
your bills and all. Take it out
on the street, you think it walks
and talks so sweet. Take it out
on the street, show it to the
heat...

BONES takes a long swig from the bottle.

                    BONES
                (continues song)
The sun is shining overhead,
there's saucers flying over our
bed. You go out on the street.
Watch 'em walk so sweet, sweet,
sweet. Watch 'em walk so sweet on
the street.
          Take back the night, honey.
Take back the night, child. Take
back the night, take back the
night, honey, take back the night,
child.
          Take back your life... Take
back your life...
          Go out on the street, see you
walk so sweet, cruising down the
street...

LEGS gets up from the table and exits to the
streete to try and earn her keep. ROCKER gets
up on the little stage and sings while PUNK and
FOLKIE play backup.

                    ROCKER
              (singing "Underground")
Hear the sounds rolling all
around. See the sounds rolling
all around. Hear the music, how
it plays through the underground,
underground, underground...

ROCKER (cont.)
In the underground, that's where
the blues sound. In the
underground, that's where the
music's made. Hear the jazz sound
all around in the undergound.
Jazz is made in the underground...
Rock and roll coming through.
Rock and roll and punk rock, too.
Everything from the underground,
underground, the underground...
Hide out in the underground,
hide out in the underground, we're
hiding out in the underground...
Where Golden Outfit is the
king, and Lady Crystal is his
queen. They rule the kingdom of
the streets. Over the children
they reign supreme. Underground,
underground, underground.
Nothing's ever as it might seem in
the underground, where life is but
a dream of yesterdays now passed
away...
Life is but a dream...
Death, just another scene, just
another part of life's dream drama
play of slow ballet...

FADE TO BLACK AS:

...piano music of Gail's Blues sounds.

END ACT II

ACT III

Scene 1:

Night on the San Francisco street. The stage is illuminated with neon lights coming from backdrops illustrating bars, liquor stores, nightclubs.

LEGS is dance-step walking, almost trotting down the street, looking for anyone she might know. For awhile "Gail's Blues" plays in time to LEGS' stride, then the music changes to that of the prelude to "Market Street"...into the piano melody of the song LEGS is about to sing to herself while walking down the street. She's dressed like a punk-rocker, in black with a chain for a belt and a rhinestone collar around her neck.

A paper cut-out of a raggedy man stands near the back of the set.

> LEGS
> (singing part of "Market Street")
> Walking through the streets of
> night, I see concrete shadows
> dancing in front of me. Jukebox
> melodies send messages out to
> me...
> We hurry down the steps,
> skipping to the beats of the
> guitar sounds, jumping through the
> refrains sounding along Memory
> Lane...sounding along Memory
> Lane...

                    LEGS (cont.)
Music blares out through the
night, calling to the angels
everywhere. Music wails into the
night, as street musicians play.
Kids strut by, looking for a jay,
wearing chains and collars, the
fashions of the day...
           (to cutout man)
      Hey, man, you got a jay?
Hey, man, you got some smoke
today?

A fade-out of light on the cut-out man, who is
replaced by PUNK, who lights a cigarette and
smokes it, sharing with LEGS.

              LEGS & PUNK
   (singing part of "Market Street")
   Standing on Market Street, smoking
   in the Warfield, yeah... Standing
   on Market Street, smoking in the
   Warfield...
      Across the street we see old
   winos dropping like flies,
   dropping like flies. In People's
   Park they sit all day, they cop
   all night, they share their wine,
   they share their wine, all the
   time...
      There's junkies all over;
   they're dropping like flies in the
   streets of the city. They're
   wasting away from the lives we
   have to live every day...

                LEGS
             (to PUNK)
It's sad to see... It's sad to
see the old ones go...

PUNK
(nodding)
There ain't no lives here anymore.
It sometimes seems it could be
kinder. Music sounds throughout
the city. You can feel the beat.
And the heat's busting all over
the street.
Famous poets stagger through
the doors of lost retreats.
There's people tripping on the
concrete, looking for something to
score. Yeah, there's street
musicians and they're blowing
their rhymes out through horns of
cosmic design...

PUNK & LEGS
(singing "Street Musicians")
Street musicians, playing in the
park. Street musicians, out for a
lark. Street musicians, playing
rhymes to the sky.
(dancing around the street together, singing)
Night time cafés sound the
blues, make me play to the sky...
Remembering the alleys, shadows
and shades, remembering
yesterdays...

LEGS
(putting her hand on PUNK's arm)
We're watching the flowers grow.
We're lost in a dream of a few
lifetimes ago, watching the
flowers grow.

PUNK
(nodding sagely; chanting "The People's Song")
Some people, they drink too much.
They fall down and get crushed.
Other people, they shoot too much.

                    PUNK (cont.)
They fall down and never get up.
     Other people, sleeping in
doorways, asking for change for
coffee. There's all kinds of
people, hanging out in front of
the free and holy restaurants; all
kinds of people, hanging out on
Market Street, playing
instruments, passing out
leaflets...

                    LEGS
(also nodding, wide-eyed and solemn; chanting)
     Oh, it sounds so sweet. I go by
and read the graffiti scrawled all
over the walls of the city. I'd
like to make a movie of the
graffiti scrawled all over the
walls of the city...

                    PUNK
                 (chanting)
It's a blue jazz wail of the
twentieth century. It's the folk
song of the city, the voice of
urbanity, the graffiti on the
walls of the city...
     Sing the graffiti on the
walls of the city. Sing the
graffiti on the walls of the
city...

                    LEGS
                 (chanting)
Gravity is the fourth dimension.
Low riders rule, high riders are
cool...

                    PUNK
                (chanting)
        Yeah, the atomic bomb was a
        mistake. Said the atomic bomb was
        a mistake. Turned the twentieth
        century into a wake...

THE GRIM REAPER comes out of the night, clad in
a long black cloak with a hood enshrouding his
face.

                THE GRIM REAPER
                (in a ghostly voice)
        Legs...

THE GRIM REAPER then rushes toward LEGS AND
PUNK, who take off down the street.

                LEGS & PUNK
        We're running, running from a gun
        into the midnight sun.

The lights dim on the action and then...

                        ...SLAM TO BLACK...

...making it look as though the characters were
all swallowed by the shadows of the night.

Music from offstage sounds...the piano sounding
like running along Market Street...

Scene 2:

People's Park at night. A lavender/purple haze
hangs over the area.

PUNK and LEGS come running into view from around
a corner. A medieval sound march plays until
the two arrive at the park, slumping into a park
bench seat at a table, across from where BONES
and JAY are sipping wine and smoking. BONES is
wearing the same black cloak as THE GRIM REAPER

was, with the hood pulled back. ROCKER and
FOLKIE are practicing on their guitars on the
little stage.

BONES wanders over to LEGS and offers her a
cigarette, which she gratefully accepts. BONES
sits down between LEGS and PUNK. PUNK puts his
head down on her shoulder and goes to sleep.

                    LEGS
          (chanting "The People's Song")
          I see all over the city there's
          people sleeping on park benches,
          people living in old cars,
          wandering the streets of the city,
          panhandling change for coffee...
               I see so many people sick and
          dying on the streets from
          malnutrition, starvation, poverty,
          neglect, abuse, disease...
               There's people hanging around
          the underground with nothing to do
          but get stoned. Nothing to do but
          be dead...

PUNK wakes up, sees BONES, JAY, ROCKER and
FOLKIE listening to LEGS tell of her obsessions.

                    PUNK
               (chanting)
          Yeah, it's hard times that we see
          all around. It's depression
          wandering everywhere. The city's
          filled with gypsies. The streets
          are the homes of children. The
          missions and the soup kitchens try
          to feed the hungry...
               It's hard times, hard times,
          hard times that I see all around
          me. What's become of our
          humanity? Why can't we love each
          other naturally?

                    PUNK (cont.)
        Why can't we help each other to
        see? There's so much emphasis on
        money. We gotta learn to help
        each other naturally. We gotta
        learn to share, or pretty soon
        there won't be nothing but death
        wandering around here...

    BONES, LEGS, PUNK, ROCKER, JAY & FOLKIE
            (in ghostly chorus chanting)
        We gotta learn to share, we gotta
        learn to care about each other.
    (passing cigarettes and wine back and forth)
                Or pretty soon there won't be
        nothing but death wandering around
        here...   Yeah, there won't be
        nothing but death wandering around
        here...   Yeah, there won't be
        nothing but death wandering around
        here...
                If we don't learn to care
        about each other, if we don't
        learn to share...there won't be
        nothing but death left here...

A gentle rain begins to fall to wash away the
pain of the street people. JAY wakes up and,
along with BONES, LEGS, PUNK, ROCKER and FOLKIE,
walk up the street to the Warfield Theater's
entrance, where they can find shelter from the
rain.

As they walk, we hear piano and piano harp music
from offstage.

                            FADE TO BLACK:

Scene 3:

Entrance of the Warfield Theater. JAY, BONES,
LEGS, ROCKER, PUNK and FOLKIE are playing guitar
and singing.

JAY, BONES, LEGS, PUNK, ROCKER & FOLKIE
There's lines everywhere.
Everywhere we see lines of people
waiting in front of us...
  Jobs, jobs, people need jobs,
paychecks and love. People need
lots of love...
  We're in a depression. We've
got the empty pocket blues...the
empty pocket blues. We're in a
depression is the only news...
  There's lines everywhere.
Everywhere we see lines of people
waiting in front of us. We're in
a depression. We've got the empty
pocket blues... The empty pocket
blues. We're in a depression is
the only news. We've got the
empty pocket blues.

VERY SLOW FADE TO BLACK

Instrumental background sound of piano and piano
harp playing offstage. We hear the rattle of
the   tambourine   as   CLIO   appears,   singing
"Hiroshima, Nagasaki, 1945."   LEGS and BONES
sing their "Spare Change" and "Wall Street"
blues routine from earlier...

END ACT III

FINIS

SPACE VISIONS,

or,
CHANSON A DIEU

THE STORY OF TWO ARTISTS OF THE LATTER PART OF THE 20TH CENTURY

This is the story of two artists coming of age in the last part of the twentieth century. It is about life lived through a series of hallucinations, as the writer Jade attempts to find her place in a world which seems to have lost its place. Searching through history, reaching out to close friend, teacher and peers, and finally looking deeply inside her own exquisite intellect, the young artist in the end derives a philosophy to guide her into the future, whatever it may hold.

lie
about reality, of midnight coming down, wandering on
lsd through the streets of China Town...

alone...
unprotected and stoned! Lie kid, just lie, then no one
will know the price you've paid...don't give any
secrets

away...about the purge of fire, the reason for disembowel-
ment, the cost of the hire, and it's still too early
to retire...

CAST:

PHAETON   A boy's voice, the symbol of a fallen bird; in mythology, he tried to drive his father's car...and burned the Earth instead

DEATH   A shadowy silhouette with a voice

JADE   A young musician with words

JASPER   A painter of impressions

TEACHER   An older confidant of JADE

POET   friend of JASPER and JADE

PAINTER   friend of JASPER and JADE

CHORUS   Five celestial musicians; the above-described characters who, in Act III, become members of the Angel Band, on the surreal planet

SETS:

Prologue   A moment in time, with dim lighting
Act 1   A moment in time
Act 2   The Fantasy Garret
Act 3   A surreal planet
Act 4   The Dada Café

PROLOGUE

JADE is seen in silhouette on the same set as used in Act I, with her guitar, singing softly "The Reaper, Death" (an old folk song).

> JADE
> There is a reaper men call Death,
> and God has given him power.
> The blade he is whetting,
> sharp, sharper, it's growing, soon
> will he be mowing, all must fall
> before him.
> Beware, o lovely flower.

There is a musical interval during which JADE changes her position and then sings "Delicate Cameo" to the flower in the vase on the table at which she is sitting.

> JADE
> (sings "Delicate Cameo")
> Death, such a sweetly fragile,
> delicate cameo, exquisitely
> textured in transparent gems...
> Death is peace, death is
> sweet, death is; what is, is...
> Death is the divinity that wanders
> everywhere.
> But now, the world of fairy-
> tales and dolls distracts me, for
> children once again embrace me, as
> the fantasies merge into mystic
> mists of satinesque lace curtains,
> enveloping me...

                    JADE (cont.)
The silhouettes whisper with the
harlequins, dwelling behind the
mirror reflections; and as the
shadows of mimetic dance emerge to
mingle, to glance, the language of
eyes, the gestures of ballet
attract me; for through corridors,
winding as labrynthian hallways,
the spectre carries me, and as our
beings merge, time drifts away
invisibly...

Silhouette lights dim as the voice of PHAETON
sounds. DEATH's voice is masculine, but of a
light texture perhaps. While JADE and TEACHER
dance in silhouette, DEATH (OPTICAL EFFECT)
appears as a shadow and floats about the stage,
while the songs sound from the wings.

                    PHAETON (O.S.)
Upon emergence into space, one
spends time wandering through
psychic corridors of laughter and
tears, until suspension of feeling
limits intervals of consciousness
to moments of amused sadness, when
time is but an entity of
fluctuating light...

                    DEATH (O.S.)
We love the children of the sun,
the shadows, silhouettes, and
shades which usher in the days,
while strewing colors along their
way; and as the flowers of light
fall randomly upon the
environments of the planets of the
solar systems, we remember the
sun, we love the sun, the texture
of its touch, the magic of its
light. We love the sun, the kiss
of its caress as its rays
illuminate the day.

             DEATH (O.S) cont.
     We love the sun, and the way it
     travels through the sky, as though
     Phaeton were once again creating
     his lullaby...

                         FADE TO BLACK AS:

...musical interlude from the orchestra begins
to play.

                  END PROLOGUE

ACT I

Lights come up to pale-blue focus and we see
JADE seated at the table with TEACHER. They
have a spoken or sung dialogue...

                    JADE
          Tell me...what was the Second
          World War like? I hadn't been
          born yet, but you know. Was it
          like the Third World War?

                    TEACHER
          No. The Second World War was
          different. It was something we
          could all touch. We knew who we
          were killing then...
               The Second World War was
          definite...not like the one going
          on today.

                    JADE
          I'm caught in the middle, and seem
          to be unable to communicate with
          other people. They never
          understand.
               I have a choice: Either
          being a hermit, recluse, vagrant,
          transient gypsy, or someone's
          lackey...

                    TEACHER
          Why don't you become your own
          lackey?

                    JADE
          That's what I'm trying to do.
          Yesterday, there was a cocktail
          party. I missed it.

TEACHER
If that's indicative of your
future...

JADE
It probably is. I suppose I must
bomb.

TEACHER
(sings "All That Matters")
All that matters is the work. All
that really matters is the work.
All that really matters is the
work, honey, baby, child...
     Sell your brain and make some
gold. Stake your claim, then turn
around and look again. You've
learned a style, honey, baby,
child...
     You want to save the world.
Sell your brain and make some
gold, make some gold, make some
gold, honey, baby, child...
     The game's the same wherever
you go. Now do you know, now do
you know, honey, baby, child...
     Sell your brain and make some
gold, make some gold, make some
gold, make some gold, honey, baby,
child...
     You want to save the world.
Sell your brain and make some
gold. Stake your claim, then turn
around and look again. You've
played the game, you've acquired a
style, honey, baby, child. Honey,
baby, child. Honey, baby,
child...
     Stake your claim, you've
played the game...

JADE
I used to think the "Drawing Room"
conversation could be left to
others. This ineptness is a sign
of the times, and of the
illiteracy that's becoming more
and more prevalent. Do people
talk here?

TEACHER
The world is bleak. Do people
talk anywhere any more? What is
there to say? It seems that the
only valuable words are those
conveying information. When the
poetry is gone, only messages
communicating explanations are
acceptable.

JADE
When life is reduced to the
accumulation of objects, what else
is there?

TEACHER
I'm presently caught in the middle
of the web of mythology, mysticism
and economics.

JADE
Economics is the only thing that
matters.

TEACHER
How can you say that?

JADE
Because that's the way the world
is. That's the way the world is.
That's the way the world is! Will
people ever change? I'm glad I'm
dead.

The tinkle of coins is heard as the song "For the Grateful Dead" is sung by JADE and TEACHER as a dialogue aria duet.

                    TEACHER
          Is one ever strange to paradise?

                    JADE
          Where have all the people gone?

                    TEACHER
          While life lasted, we lived for
          others.

                    JADE
          Now, after death, we live for
          ourselves.

                    TEACHER
          Speak to me in pictures and I'll
          answer you in song.

                    JADE
          Dream of me in colors, caress me
          with electricity.

                    TEACHER
          Why were we so pitiful while
          waiting so patiently for our souls
          to arrive?

                    JADE
          Why were we as broken birds, lost
          in memories of flights long past?

                    TEACHER
          Shock me into outer space...

                    JADE
          ...and I'll find a planet of
          escape.

                    TEACHER
Now that sanctuary has been
caught, we float through our days
in silhouette. Build for me an
opera...

                    JADE
...and we'll be a symphony.

                JADE & TEACHER
While life lasted, we lived for
others. Now, after death, we live
for ourselves.

                    JADE
Feed me with ideas, love me with
philosophy...

                    TEACHER
...and we'll dance in poetry.

                JADE & TEACHER
Live with me a ballet. While life
lasted, we lived for others. Now,
after death, we live for
ourselves. We live for
ourselves... Is one ever strange
to paradise? Where have all the
people gone?

                        FADE TO BLACK AS:

JADE and TEACHER are seen as silhouettes dancing
together on the stage, as before.

                    END ACT I

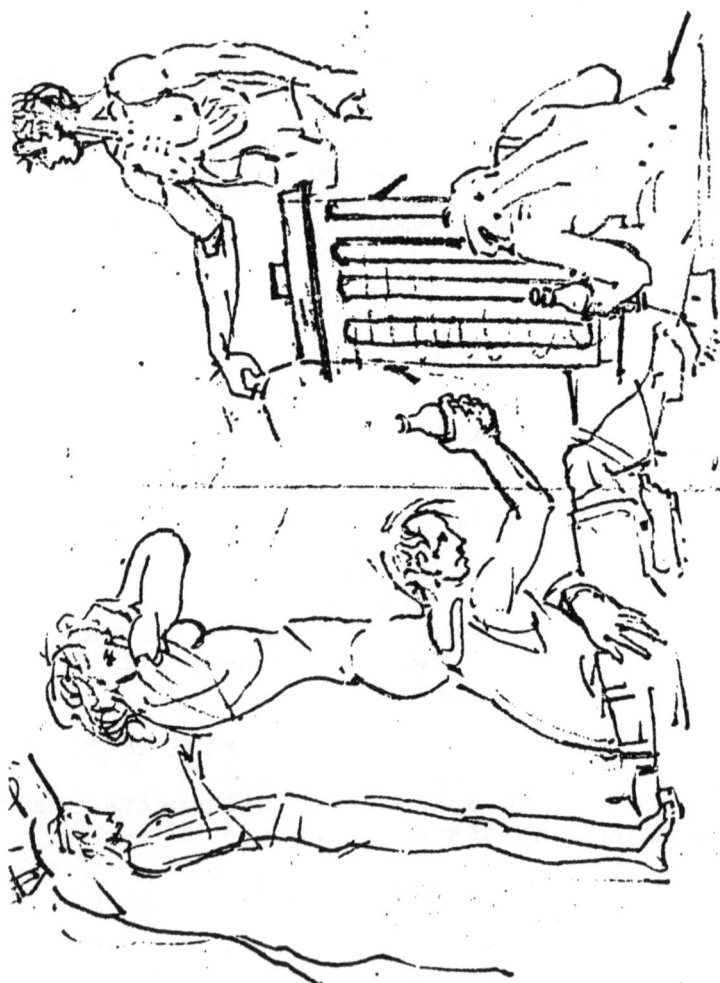

ACT II

JASPER's fantasy artist's garret. As the lights
rise, JADE is seen strumming the guitar while
sitting in a turquoise armchair, either singing
or talking "Metamorphosis" as though in
conversation with JASPER, the painter. JASPER
is pasting pictures on a collage set upon a
zodiac frame balanced on an easel. It is early
in the morning.

> JADE
> (sings "Metamorphosis")
> Twenty after four in the morning,
> sitting in a turquoise chair,
> watching twelfth-century pedestals
> crumbling, thirteenth-century
> cathedrals burning, fourteenth-
> century children crying,
> fifteenth-century people dying,
> sixteenth-century minds exploding
> into expressions of illumination,
> seventeenth-century kingdoms
> tumbling, eighteenth-century
> revolutions liberating,
> nineteenth-century inventions
> breaking chains of slavery...as
> twentieth-century wars and
> depressions bridge the ground for
> lost souls, explorations of
> consciousness, causing visionary
> scientists to transmit magic
> mystic music beams through
> translucent crystals of precious
> metals into space...

JADE (cont.)
Twenty after four in the morning,
sitting in a turquoise chair,
thinking of metamorphosis,
thinking of the velvet
underground, which, while
caressing with electricity,
exchanges minds indifferently,
based upon the connection...for
madness is contagious when
pantomimes and cybernetic rhymes
of colors sing the answers to the
questions of the sages, and
creators' ideas change the course
of history's pages...

JADE fades off into instrumental strumming only
while JASPER ponders her painting.

JASPER
(pensively)
What if all photographs are really
alive, and sometimes the
characters inhabiting them come
out into the world to do things
for persons in distress...then,
when the person's problem is
solved, the character from the
photograph returns to the
photograph and becomes just an
image again?

JADE
Oh, yes. I think that some
photographic worlds also tell
celluloid stories, for some
artists, while pursuing therapy,
are entering dimensions of psychic
intensity. Cameras' reflections
capture light, recreating sight.

> JASPER

I think news is boring because it
seems that, while children dance
energy away hopelessly, women try
to make their way, helplessly...

> JADE
> (looks at JASPER wryly)

You're being awfully profound this
morning! Ha-ha!

JASPER breaks into a dance step and dances about
the stage gracefully as though an Isadora Duncan
in veils, and she sings as though a children's
song...

> JASPER

Earth, ecology, radar, people...
Hello, people who love people.
Yesterday is tomorrow wherever one
may be, and some children have
everything going...
> (changes voice, more sophisticated)

Work is the most important
thing. I always admired Jean
Genet, for the only thing that
saved him was his work. Work is
the most important thing.

> JADE
> (sings "St. Genet")

Genet, sweet Genet, Sartre called
you saint. Genet, sweet Genet,
now I've also seen the hate.
Genet was a thief, now I know why.
Genet was a cheat, now I know why.
Genet, Saint Genet, Jean
Genet, orphan, prisoner, criminal,
some say... Genet, sweet Genet,
pourquoi Genet, Saint Genet...

> JASPER

I've always liked Rimbaud also.

                    JADE
          (sings "Arthur Rimbaud")
     Arthur Rimbaud, how long ago did
     you live? How long ago did you
     die? Arthur Rimbaud, how long ago
     did you cry, did you sigh for your
     ideals?
          Arthur Rimbaud, vagabond poet
     of an age ago, you've been so
     often duplicated; François Villon,
     Charles Baudelaire, Genet, sweet
     Genet, da, dada, da, da dada, da
     da, dadadada, da...

JADE and JASPER now dance a music-box minuet,
bending parts of their anatomy as the bass notes
sound, for they are as marionettes with broken
strings...

After the dance, cartoon slides flash as
backdrop to "The Fairy Tale," which JADE plays
and sings while JASPER goes back to her collage,
pasting pieces of paper on the surface of the
painting on the zodiac frame.

                    JADE
          (sings "The Fairy Tale")
     While Charlie Chaplin flirts with
     the crow, Teddy Bear hangs out at
     Jack in the Box, street kids in
     silhouette wander past the park,
     and War Baby, who once followed
     Tambourine Man, now rides a wooden
     rocking horse. A wooden rocking
     horse, for the psychedelic clown
     is dancing with the tiger.
          The sad prince sits in his
     costume of red and blue at a table
     and quietly stares. The people's
     princess grins, for she really
     knows...

JADE (cont.)
The sad prince babbles behind his
round glasses, of war, of desires,
adventures and deaths, of jousts,
tortures, trials and fires, of
courts and jesters, alchemy and
Rosicrucians' preciously secret,
jeweled society...

JASPER
(also sings "The Fairy Tale")
The people's princess, dressed in
blue, sits before a table of toys
in the house of forgotten years
and watches visions of meadows, of
picnics, of goblets, and song, of
troubadors and traveling shows.
She watches, she listens to the
tales, riddles and rhymes of
magicians, describing
resurrections, deaths and
transmutations...
     The people's princess listens
to the words, the explanations,
the musical presentations,
attempting to understand the
beauty she sees all around her.
     The beauty of crystal, of
cameo, of porcelain, of harmony,
the beauty she sees all around
her...

JASPER dances for a while, then stops to talk.

JASPER
Let's start a movement that
everything might someday be
beautiful...

JADE

Or is everything already
beautiful? For to be surreal
while projecting mystique upon the
city streets is theater today...

JASPER and JADE begin to sing as slides of the
people mentioned flash on the walls, and the
environment is soon that of a celluloid carnival
about which the two characters dance in slow
ballet.

JADE & JASPER
(sing "The Chant of 20th Century Names")
Salvador Dali, Antoine Artaud,
Jean Cocteau, Gertrude Stein,
Alice B. Toklas, Picasso,
Apollinaire, Igor Stravinsky, Erik
Satie, Maurice Ravel, Claude
Debussy, Andre Breton, Jean Genet,
Arthur Rimbaud, are you still
wandering about today? It
sometimes seems that way...

JADE
(sings "The Painter's Song")
This morning, I cried for Gertrude
Stein, while grinning with Picasso
and imitating Charlie Chaplin,
visualizing Cocteau and Colette
laughingly conferring over
absinthe...
      This morning, a silver,
translucent Salvador Dali moon
floated through an El Greco sky,
as Aubrey Beardsley's tree shadows
silhouetted the freezing pre-dawn
time, and Vincent van Gogh's
flowers and meadows surrounded my
mind's eye; as memories of
Matisse's seaside scenes flashed
before me, regret for a past world
enveloped me.

JADE (cont.)
This morning, Shakespeare sang to
me, while the shades of
Michelangelo and Leonardo wandered
beside me, as Dante and Virgil led
the way...
But now fog and mist, with
ocean spray, camouflage the
velvet-cloaked characters of
yesterday.

JASPER
(talking)
But, from another dimension,
Bertold Brecht seems to be the
current fashion...

JADE
Is everyone becoming another? Is
it possible?

JASPER
It is highly possible that they
are...

JADE
(sings "The Writer's Song")
After writers, directors, actors
and painters, after love, after
death, after religion and
demonstration, after
confrontation, negotiation and
exploration of the dialectic...
After veils of faces seen
through mists of hallucinations,
after men, after women, after
children and revolutions, after
Bach, after Beethoven, baroque and
art nouveau, after the
impressionists, the futurists, the
cubists, the dadaists, and
surrealists, after Gertrude Stein,
Pablo Picasso and Noel Coward, is
there anything?

VERY SLOW FADE TO BLACK AS:

                    JASPER
Love is recognition, someone said.
Work is a necessity, I once read.

                    JADE
Circles, squares, triangles,
cubes, dots and lines in gem
design dance all around as bolts
of electric notes swirl in
chromatic time, outlining
labyrinths of synchronistic
design.
        While children pursue
fantasy...fantasy, illusion, is
there a reality, as the computer's
voice describes dots, lines,
cubes, spheres, triangles, cones
and domes, light rays from
kaleidescopic prisms refine
contemporary ways...
        Jade sways all around, all
around, looking for comedy, having
exhausted tragedy; Jade on Mercury
wanders hermetically, while living
with color and sound...
        Color and sound, they are
such total beings. Color and
sound can do so many things.
Color and sound, lightwaves and
currents floating up and down...

                END ACT II

ACT III

Lights and blue flames flicker through and about a fantastical world of octagonal, strangely dimensional structures. Musical instruments are set about the stage. JADE dances in colors, as the angelic CHORUS wanders in ballet movement.

> JADE
> (sings "Being")
> Listen to the sound of sight, feel
> the scent of the night, touch the
> texture of the air, be the myth of
> eternal light...
> Love the kiss of the sun,
> love the stream of grass blades
> upon which to run, love the mist
> of summer breeze's caress, love
> the faded petals of forgotten
> flowers...
> Long for open, empty, endless
> spaces, long for infinite
> dimensions, long for harmony, for
> peace, for remembrance of
> antiquity, long for truth, for
> graciousness, for hope, for
> agelessness, for beauty, for
> posterity, for order, for
> infinity...

The CHORUS dances a celebration of music and future music.

> CHORUS
> (sings "Future Music")
> Future music paints bright colors,
> as prancing flowers pattern in
> gypsy children games...

                    CHORUS (cont.)
Future music portrays motions,
foretells man's moods, illustrates
rhythms of a planet soon uniting,
of future people flying, while
activating shadows, translucent
and silhouette, in lavender and
purple...
          All shall act as children
once again...
          Future music completely
portrays the dream, who would
interpret what is seen, who would
define what such things mean...
          Future music flashing before
eyes blinking, who would interpret
what is seen, who would define
what such things mean...

JADE conducts; three members of the CHORUS pick
up instruments and play; two of them dance a
surreal ballet with JADE.

                    JADE
               (sings "Omega")
The battered outline, fractured
shape-filled almost-hues now
populate the lakes of night...
          That yesterday might be
undone, that poetry might stir the
air, that metronomes keep time...
          With strokes of silver,
raindrop, tinkle chime, that
knowledge be dispensed, that
gentle tenderness be suggested in
a mild caress, that humanity be
recognized instead of analyzed...

The remaining two CHORUS members pick up
instruments and play. JADE dances and sings.

                    JADE
          (still sings "Omega")
When humor can be revived, when
laughter can be caught, when
time's threads can be re-sought,
then we shall return to the land
of the actors, the land of the
stage, the plan of the sage, the
clan of the coming age...

JADE continues to dance.

                   CHORUS
          (sings "The Mystic")
Oh, Muse of fire, beam of light,
vibrations of Minerva dance into
electric sight, as sounds of
swaying lavender, purple, blue and
green music beams flash off walls,
swell the halls...
     The pantomimes of clown
musicians sway the age, while
prancing in time to cybernetic
rhyme; madness is contagious when
unseen colors sing the answers to
the sages, and unimagined,
unthought, unknown ideas change
the course of history's patterned
pages...

                   CHORUS
(sings "Music Bouncing Off the Walls")
     Music bouncing off the walls,
electric lights blink round as
vibrations stretch the air...
     Coloring softly, we flash
here, sultry light shades float
by, we stare as circus characters
abound...
     Floating spring-soft air
surrounds, different faces,
chanting eyes, captured Moon Man
tunes us high...

CHORUS (cont.)
Music bouncing off the walls,
electric lights pirouetting now,
flashing colors, flashing sound,
activating words resound...
    Recharging flowers falling
down, resurrection has just
begun...
    Resurrection has just begun,
as golden rubies complement silver
pearls, while purple emeralds
beside copper green diamonds float
into corrals of red iron,
surrounded by blue topaz, flashing
black sapphires of opalized
streams of radium...
    Jade and Jasper are together
once again, and, as Earth revolves
slowly, we see bolts of
electricity whirling through
space...
    For the children from the
blue planet are playing with the
necklace of faces. The diamonds
are scattering rhinestones, the
opals are dissolving
incandescently, the emeralds are
flashing meteors, the rubies are
exploding comets, the amethysts
are becoming jade mirrors...
    And now that the pearls are
returning to cosmic sand, the
sapphires, prisms of electricity,
are dancing through reflections of
topaz wavelengths into radiant
light...
    Music bouncing off the walls,
electric lights blink 'round as
vibrations stretch the air...
    Coloring softly, we flash
here, sultry light-shades float
by, we stare, as circus characters
abound...

CHORUS (cont.)
Floating spring-soft air
surrounds, different faces,
chanting eyes, captured Moon Man
tunes us high...
    Music bouncing off the walls,
electric lights pirouetting now,
flashing colors, flashing sound,
activating words resound...
    Recharging flowers falling
down...
    Resurrection has just
begun...
    Resurrection, metamorphosis,
resurrection...
    Resurrection, metamorphosis,
resurrection...
    Resurrection, resurrection,
resurrection...
    Resurrection...

FADE TO BLACK AS:

CHORUS is seen in silhouette, still dancing and
playing and singing...

END ACT III

ACT IV

JADE plays the guitar in the window of The Dada Café, while on the street below JASPER sings and wanders around outside the window. POET and PAINTER are sitting together at a table in the café.

> JASPER
> (sings "The Sun Rises")
> After the sun rises, noon dances
> through sky circuses of evening
> tears, and the dream drama days of
> slow ballet fade into decades of
> symphonic centuries...
> For after the sun rises, noon
> dances through sky circuses of
> evening tears...

The sound of JADE's music can be heard faintly in the street, subdued by JASPER's song.

> JASPER
> (sings "The Contents of Your Mind")
> Have you ever seen the contents of
> your mind flashing as a film upon
> the sky?
> Have you ever seen the
> stories of your life unfolding as
> television scenes before your
> eyes?
> Have you ever seen all the
> people that you are chase each
> other across your face as though
> they were in a race?

JASPER (cont.)
Have you ever gone inside your
brain and, after wandering around,
turned around, come stumbling,
staggering, tumbling back out
again?
        Have you ever seen the
buildings of the city dance while
the streets rippled to a rhythm of
their own?
        Have you ever seen such
things with your eyes?
        When I take the time to look,
I see that the faces on the clouds
have again returned to me, and I
love these faces, for they explain
the visions of history that I see
flashing before my eyes, and at
such times, I see a light shining
through the night...

JASPER enters the café, sits down at the table
with POET and PAINTER.   JADE plays melodies.
JASPER extends her hand, which has a sparkling
ring on one of her fingers.

                    JASPER
            (sings "The Ring Song")
Look into my ring. See the spires
of the castles. Do you see the
mist of cobweb skies? Can you
hear the voices as they call me?
        I ran away, but only for a
day. Look into my ring. There's
a magic place somewhere, I
sometimes go there. I came here
from there. When I'm not here,
I'm there...
        Look into my ring. Perhaps
I'll take you to my land with me.
Perhaps I'll love you. Would you
like to come with me? Look into
my ring...

                    POET
              (interrupts; chants)
You're perfect at this moment. At
this perfect moment, you're
perfect; you're you...
         Why not accept it? You've
evolved to it and will go beyond
it. But at this moment, don't you
see, how you're perfectly you?
         Isn't it magnificent? Isn't
it grand? What's so difficult?
Why not accept the fact that
you're perfect at this moment?
Isn't it true that you're
perfectly you?

JASPER continues to look at her ring, flips a
tiny spring and the top pops open. She places
her fingertip inside the cavity and captures a
blue square of paper, ever so tiny. She extends
her fingertip toward the middle of the table so
POET and PAINTER might see the small piece of
paper.

                   JASPER
Orange sunshine, purple micro-dot,
white lightning, clear light,
orange wedges, electric Kool-aid,
unicorn purple, blues, LSD 50, LSD
25...Mickey Mouse, Owsley tabs...
         Come on, let's trip together,
we'll exchange worlds, and if you
like my mind, well then, you'll be
mine...
         (looks around room in awe)
         I never knew. I never knew.
I never knew...

                    PAINTER
                   (to POET)
Don't waste words on her. Can't
you see she doesn't even hear what
you say? She doesn't care. She's
happy being out of her mind. She
likes being lost somewhere out
there...

                    JASPER
I never knew it would be like
this. I never thought I would
trip like this. This time I've
really blown my mind. I never
knew. I never knew. I never
knew. I never knew...

                    JADE
        (sings "The Castle Song")
Now that the knight has returned
to the castle, the crusade having
been played through, only the
checkmate to end the game of chess
remains. But we have not yet come
to that cue, for now is but a mist
of charade and innuendo, of haiku
and medieval madrigal...
        Only the checkmate to end the
game of chess remains...
        But we have not yet come to
that cue...

                    JASPER
        (looks at her companions)
I never knew. I never knew it
would be like this. I never knew.
I never knew. I never knew...

JADE and JASPER lock eyes for a moment.

JADE
(sings "We've Got To Love Each Other")
We've got to love each other if
we're going to survive...
We've got to help each other
want to stay alive...
We've got to like each other,
even when we don't...

JASPER, POET & PAINTER
(also sing)
We've got to love each other if
we're going to survive...
We've got to help each other
want to stay alive...
We've got to like each other,
even when we don't...

JADE
(still singing)
We've got to love each other if
we're going to survive
We've got to help each other
want to stay alive...
We've got to like each other,
even when we don't...

JADE, JASPER, POET & PAINTER
We've got to love each other...
We've got to help each
other...
We've got to like each other
if we're to survive...

JASPER
(looks into ring again; sings "The Ring Song")
Look into my ring. See the spires
of the castles. Do you see the
mist of cobweb skies? Can you
hear the voices as they call me?
I ran away, but only for a
day. Look into my ring. There's
a place, a magic land inside my
ring.

                    JASPER (cont.)
I sometimes go there. I came here
from there. When I'm not here,
I'm there...
         Look into my ring. Perhaps
I'll take you to my land with me.
Perhaps I'll love you. Would you
like to come with me? Look into
my ring...

JASPER rises from the table and heads out the
door of the café to dance on the sidewalk. POET
and PAINTER follow her. The three appear to
talk together and share cigarettes. JASPER
wanders away, looking up at the sky...

                    JASPER
       (sings "Hello, Moon, Hello, Stars")
         Hello, moon. Hello, stars.
         Hello, solar system. As I see the
         way you're all positioned, I must
         admit that God's the best Artist
         of us all...
              I love the way the sky looks
         at night, when the stars are
         silhouetted through a mist of
         light, and Venus, lingering close
         by, shines bright.
              I love the touch of the wind,
         the universe of galaxies, the
         smiles of the dawn, the rising of
         the sun...
              While in the solar system of
         the Milky Way, the suns, the
         moons, the planets are as a
         necklace of jewels, of precious
         metals... Resurrection has just
         begun and is continuing...

JASPER, POET & PAINTER
(singing)
Resurrection, metamorphosis,
energy, energy, energy, love,
hope, tranquility...please send
Earth some energy, energy, love,
hope, tranquility, resurrection,
metamorphosis, energy, energy,
love, hope, tranquility. Earth
needs energy, energy, love, hope,
tranquility, harmony...
     Resurrection, metamorphosis,
energy, love, hope, tranquility,
harmony, resurrection,
metamorphosis, resurrection,
resurrection, resurrection,
resurrection...

JADE
(voice rising above continuing chorus)
     While the twentieth-century light
music concert plays, a symphony of
sight illuminates the harmony of
mad musicians' discordant violins,
and dream drama plays of slow
ballet complement transparent
shadows of reality, dancing
abandonly, flashing telepathically
beams of insight to the children
struggling on the rocks below...
     Time for a moment hesitates
in space, where rising moons,
projecting expressions of cavern
frowns in crescent scenes, spin
all around the blazing suns rising
above the rolling hills and
shadowy mountains of mind's
distant skies...where the
translucent days fade into
pastelized twilights of
transparent light...

JASPER, POET & PAINTER
Resurrection, metamorphosis,
energy, love, hope, tranquility,
harmony, resurrection,
metamorphosis, energy, energy,
energy, love, hope, tranquility,
harmony, metamorphosis,
metamorphosis, metamorphosis...

FADE TO BLACK AS:

...the dancing figure of JASPER fades into a
tiny distant silhouette...

END ACT IV

FINIS

1990 remembering 1968

we made it out of the alley,
over to the dark side of town, never to
return to the stash pad...
never to leave the underground...

we made it on up to a safe house,
nestling on fugitive row...
escaping into the decades, with a past
lost to all we did know...

and the beat goes round
like a circle, while the band plays in the
background...

only the words of the poets tell
of the way things went down...

when the notes of the jazz men exploded into
the soul of the times...

when the piper was playing in Frisco, when
music was a coded grapevine.

--Brio Burgess

1967 looking at 1995

standing on the corner
prancing in the scene,
    rapping to a dancing
teen's scream,

    great big shoes,
falling down pants,
    over-sized jackets,
baseball caps,
    must be some
new kind of tramps...

you can catch 'em on
the t.v. and
hear 'em on the radio,
    even on the MTV
video show...
crossing back and forth
    with authority...
telling stories for
    all to be...ain't nothing
new, wanting to be free
from responsibility...

    yeah, they the rappers,
new kind of dance hall
    chatters...talking up a
storm...screaming around
    like new babes just
born...yeah, they the rappers,
    new kind of dance hall
chatters...they the rap ap appers...

    with great big shoes,
falling down jeans,
    braids and dreadlock
curly cue creams...
    oversized jackets,
undersized means.
    hoping to win the
lottery, in their day dream
schemes...

--Brio Burgess

ABOUT THE AUTHOR

Brio Burgess is the oldest of eleven children born to artistic parents living in the San Francisco Bay area after World War II. She grew up in adversity in the midst of the city's rich cultural resources, and began to express herself early on in musical, artistic and poetic form. Surrounded by the energy of the triumphant Beat Renaissance and the budding Civil Rights Movement, Brio became a herald of the age to be brought on by her generation.

The life she led in those years is best described in the works contained in this volume. Only through a series of miracles has she survived.

At this time, Brio is living quietly in upstate New York, working in the human services field and recently attained her B.A. in Sociology from Russell Sage College. Among her interests are Eastern medicine, meditation, life extension and performance presentations of music and words.

A playwright, composer, lyricist, and member of The Dramatists' Guild, Brio's poems have been widely published and her plays produced in New York. This volume is her first full-length publication.

QUOTH THE CRITICS

"Brio Burgess writes about an America most people go through their lives not being aware of. Her stories, plays and narratives are often painfully real, poetic, touching, humorous and hold up a mirror for America to see itself. Jack [Kerouac] always told me to search for the diamond in the sidewalk. Brio Burgess helps us down this road which few have travelled."
> --David Amram, composer for
> *Splendor in the Grass*, *The Manchurian Candidate*,
> *Young Savages* and *Pull My Daisy*

"Brio Burgess is super-contemporary. Her works are phoenix birds for all who have arisen, and for those yet to rise."
> --Jane Mayhall, poet

"A 'happening.'"
> --Max Lifchitz, composer

"Brio Burgess...uses live visual imagery married to musical sounds..."
> --Ron Emery, *Albany Times Union*

"After reading the works in this volume, I was reminded of *The Lower Depths* by Maxim Gorky. ... While I've never seen Brio Burgess' work performed, I believe these pieces can work very well on the stage and hope to see these plays produced."
> --Furumi Sano, writer/reviewer

"...the Californian reality revolution of the sixties and seventies."
                    --Rod Summers, VEC Audio Exchange

"I didn't live through the '60s and only remember the '70s through childhood memories with no exposure to the kinds of things Brio Burgess writes about until I reached college. But the problems of teenage runaways and drugs are important ones which need to be dealt with...and soon! We can save our kids if everyone cares and lends a hand...and Brio Burgess has taken her own personal step with this book!"
                    --Jonathan Athos, poet/writer

"Her shows are always a mystical, ethereal delight."
                    --Artists for a New Politics

"If I were homeless, I'd want Brio Burgess to write about me!"
                    --Kevin S. Birnbaum
        former editor of *The Grapevine News* (Phoenix)
            and writer/director of *Justice Be Damned*

"Brio Burgess' plays show the pain and suffering of people living on the streets...a problem which has not gone away since the 1960s and 1970s, but which continues to increase in both the numbers of people and the depth of their problems. Hopefully her work will bring to light the plight of these people...and something will be done about it, on an individual basis-- yes, by you, the person reading this book--and on a wide-scale effort."
                    --Daryl F. Mallett
        co-editor of *Imaginative Futures* and publisher
            of Angel Enterprises/Jacob's Ladder Books

www.ingramcontent.com/pod-product-compliance
Lightning Source LLC
LaVergne TN
LVHW011233080426
835509LV00005B/478